BASIC BIBLE GUIDE
DAILY DEVOTIONAL
2013 Copyright All Rights Reserved

BASIC BIBLE GUIDE'S MISSION:
Help ALL people, regardless of their beliefs; understand the Bible with a fact-based easy to use system, free of cost.
To be part of this mission, would you donate just 1 dollar a month so we can translate our website and book for people around the world?
(Basic Bible Guide is an IRS approved 501(c)(3) nonprofit, public charity.)

Please visit us at our website!
www.BasicBibleGuide.org

THANK YOU AND MANY BLESSINGS!

A special thanks to all my family and friends who helped inspire, edit, improve, encourage, and support BBG throughout these 30–plus years.
Daniel Paul Kennedy, Founder
(Visit BasicBibleGuide.org to read the Founder's true life story.)

CONTENTS

Introduction to Basic Bible Guide

1. Basic Bible Guide (BBG) is a straight forward devotional with not much flash or "entertainment", and although it is quick and easy, it is probably different than other formats you may have encountered. BBG is intended to show people what the Bible actually says. BBG is not intended to indoctrinate, teach, offer commentary or biased opinions (there are MANY programs available that will do that).

2. BBG is an overview of the entire Bible; all of its 66 separate writings/"books" are reviewed. For a much fuller understanding, it is recommended that you read the entire Bible as you go through this devotional (or as soon as you are able) from front to back (the same order the course is designed). If you can read 4 to 5 pages each week you will be able to read the whole Bible in 365 days. However; if you do not, BBG will still deliver a remarkable understanding of the Bible.

3. You will be able to answer questions, such as:
   a. What does the Bible really say, and where did it come from?
   b. Is it factual or just fairy tales?
   c. Is it relevant in today's culture?
   d. Does it answer the tough questions that I have about life?

4. Although much of the Bible is covered in this devotional you may feel that you will not retain as much as you would like, but as you continue to read the Bible, you will acquire more information.

5. Please understand if there seems to be something or various facts missing, BBG is only an overview. The majority of the Bible is not read during this devotional, and that is one of the reasons BBG recommends reading the entire Bible.

6. Also recognize, as a particular passage is read in BBG, there may be other areas of the Bible that cover the same topic. So, do not assume to have a thorough understanding of how the Bible views this topic, or that the Bible, as a whole, agrees or disagrees with what is being read. A more complete study is required to gain accurate knowledge of these topics.

7. As you go through this devotional/the Bible expect to discover insights, ideas, stories and concepts that will challenge you, be thought provoking, you may not understand, you may not agree with, or may even find offensive.

8. With this in mind, make the commitment right now to find out for yourself what the Bible actually says, and complete this entire devotional; as other books need to be read to the end in order for the reader to grasp and understand the concept in its entirety, the Bible works the same way. Remember, there are no teachings or opinions; Basic Bible Guide was designed to simply show you what the Bible declares.

Instructions for Basic Bible Guide (BBG)

1. You only need three things: 1. A Bible, preferably English Standard Version (ESV) but any Bible can be used. 2. A Basic Bible Guide: Daily Devotional book. 3. A pen for note-taking.

2. BBG consists of key scripture passages from every book of the 66 books of the Bible (which you read from your own Bible). Many of these passages are accompanied by scriptures from other places in the Bible (most going back and forth from the Old and New Testaments); these are known as "cross references".

3. **Note:** The Bible covers thousands of years of history, and is a very large book, so the cross references are considerably helpful in understanding the entire Bible. They link similar ideas, story lines, and prophetic writings, and show when and where these prophesies are fulfilled. All the cross references are noted where they are in the Bible, to assist in further study.

4. **Note:** Regarding cross references, the New Testament has these scriptures explaining the importance of the relationship between the Old and New Testaments. (Romans 15:4 "For whatever was written in former days was written for our instruction, that through endurance and through the encouragement of the Scriptures we might have hope." and I Corinthians 10:11 "Now these things happened to them as an example, but they were written down for our instruction, on whom the end of the ages has come.")

5. **Note: Not all passages have "cross references". Only the passages that have a thinner line below them are cross references intended to correspond with the passages that are above the thinner line.**

6. Read the day's devotional and write down any thoughts, questions, or insights you may have in the space provided.

7. Throughout BBG you will find **"Reminders:"** and **"Notes:"** that will assist you in understanding the sections and passages of the Bible.

General Bible Facts

1. The word "Bible" means "The Book" (in Greek - "*Ta Biblia*") implying the book of books - superior to other books.

2. There are 66 separate writings or "books" that make up the Bible. These "books" were given names to identify them, such as Genesis, John and Revelation.

3. Many books have abbreviations such as, Gen. for Genesis, Ex. for Exodus, Eph. for Ephesians, Jn. For John, and Rev. for Revelation.

4. Each book is divided into "chapters", marked with the larger number at the beginning of each chapter (unless the book has only 1 chapter, these include Obadiah, Philemon, II John, III John, and Jude).

5. Each chapter is divided into "verses", marked by the smaller number at the beginning of each verse. The book name, chapter, and verse number is known as the Bible reference or "address". One of the most well-known Bible verses/addresses is John 3:16. "For God so loved the world, that he gave his only Son, that whoever believes in him should not perish but have eternal life."

6. The Bible is divided into two main sections, the first is known as the "Old Testament" and the second is called the "New Testament".

7. These two sections are then divided into "books": 39 books in the Old Testament, and 27 books in the New Testament.

8. (Definition of "Testament")
   Webster's Dictionary:
   1. either of two main divisions of the Bible, evidence, witness
   American Heritage Dictionary:
   1. something that serves as tangible proof or evidence
   2. a statement of belief; a credo

9. **The Old Testament** is the first main section of the Bible and was originally written in the Hebrew language. It is comprised of 39 books and covers a time line in history from the creation of the World (in Genesis chapters 1 and 2) through a prophesy of God's "judgment of the wicked" and "blessing" to those who "fear" (or revere) God's name (in Malachi, Chapter 4, approximately 500 B.C.).

10. The Old Testament is the Hebrew (or Jewish) Bible (Tanakh in Hebrew).

11. The first five books of the Old Testament in Hebrew are called the Torah (meaning "law"). In Greek these first five books are called The Pentateuch, or *"The Book of the Law of the Lord"* given by Moses.

12. The next 12 books of the Old Testament are recognized as "Historical Books" because they tell the history of the Israelites (who are also known as the Hebrews or Jews), from the time of their departure from slavery in Egypt, to the reign of King Ahasuerus, who was one of the rulers of Persia (the Persians) and Media (the Medes) which is approximately an 875-year time line.

13. The next five books of the Old Testament are considered "Poetic Books" due to their writing styles. These books include:

    a. Job (is a man's name, pronounced with a long o), is mainly dialog between Job, his friends and God

    b. Psalms, which are songs (with no musical notes included on the pages)

    c. Proverbs, which are statements of wisdom and instruction

    d. Ecclesiastes, which is mainly the dissertation of a bitter and unfulfilled King

    e. Song of Solomon (also known as Song of Songs), which is a passionate dialogue between lovers

14. The next 17 books of the Old Testament are "Prophetic Books" which are written by prophets. These books are titled by the name of each of the prophets who wrote them (such as Isaiah, Jonah, and Joel). Prophets are people who convey messages to others, as they have been revealed to them by God (usually concerning the future). In these books, you will find prophesies that are later fulfilled by Jesus in the New Testament, as can be seen in the cross references.

15. **The New Testament** is the second main section of the Bible and was originally written in Greek. It is comprised of 27 books that cover the life, ministry and purpose of Jesus Christ, as well as the ministry of Jesus' first believers (also known as followers, disciples or Christians, which means "little Christ" or Christ-like). It includes letters of instruction and exhortation to the growing groups of believers around the world. The New Testament concludes with events and instructions for the end of this world and the beginning of a new world.

16. The first four books of the New Testament are known as the "Gospels", which means "good news". They cover the life of Jesus on Earth, and are written (and titled) by four different people (Matthew, Mark, Luke and John).

17. The fifth book of the New Testament is Acts, which refers to the "acts" of the Apostles (the leaders for the ministry of Jesus).

18. The next twenty-one books of the New Testament are letters to groups (or individuals) from the Apostles/leaders from Jesus (also known as Epistle's), for the purpose of: instructing, correcting, rebuking and exhorting them, as well as salutations.

19. The last book of the New Testament is Revelation (which means "unveiling"), covering the end of this world and the beginning of a new one.

20. **Note:** Many of the books and stories in the Bible overlap and/or continue where another left off. For example, Daniel starts where Jeremiah ends, Ezra continues after Daniel, Nehemiah after Ezra, I Kings and II Kings overlap in time with I Chronicles and II Chronicles. Several of the prophetic books also overlap in time. The first four books of the New Testament (The Gospels) cover the same timeline but from different writers' perspectives. Some of the Epistles are written to cities that Paul visited in the book of Acts.

21. There was a period of approximately 400 years not recorded in the Bible between the Old and New Testament known as the Intertestamental Period.

22. The Bible was written by approximately 36 different people, including a tax collector (Matthew), kings (Solomon), a doctor (Luke) and fishermen (Peter and John). It took a period of about 1,500 years to complete writing. Its first author was Moses, after the Egyptians' enslavement of the Hebrews (the book of Genesis, approximately 1475 B. C.). The last author of the Bible was John (Jesus' companion and disciple), approximately 90 A.D. (the book of Revelation).

23. **Note:** The initials B.C. in a date refer to "Before Christ", or before Jesus Christ's birth. The initials A.D. stand for the Latin phrase "Anno Domini", which translates to "the Year of Our Lord," referring to the years after the birth of Jesus Christ.

24. The Bible was the first book ever printed on a printing press and has been reprinted more than any book in history. It has also been translated into more languages than any other book.

25. The most commonly known English translation of the Bible is the King James Version (KJV) Bible or the "authorized version", authorized by King James of England in 1611 A.D. There are other versions people find easier to comprehend since the English/American language has changed since then. It is best to study several versions/translations simultaneously for a fuller understanding.

26. Some Bibles are "translations" and others are a "paraphrase". A translation is when a word or term from one language is copied "word-for-word" (as accurately as possible) to another language. A paraphrase gives the meaning of a word or passage "thought for thought". Check your Bible to find out which you have.

27. The Scripture printed in BBG is the English Standard Version (ESV) translation.

28. Depending on the type of Bible you have, you will probably notice headings before passages emphasizing the event(s) that are going to take place in the following verses. Unless there is a verse number before the text these are not part of the Bible but were added for a point of reference for the reader. Many Bibles also have letters and other symbols throughout them to signify a footnote or some other type of textual note that expands upon the Bible's text. Consult your Bible to learn what these mean.

29. **Note:** If you desire answers about or from the Bible, the best source IS the Bible—not people's traditions or philosophies. If someone cannot answer your questions from the Bible, be cautious receiving their answer.

30. There is a group of people mentioned in the Bible that were applauded for searching the Scriptures and looking up what was being told them, the Bereans.

31. Acts 17:11 "Now these Jews were more noble than those in Thessalonica; they received the word with all eagerness, examining the Scriptures daily to see if these things were so."

32. **Note:** There are many ways to "read" the Bible:
    a. A pocket sized Bible can be kept with you to read as you wait (i.e. at the doctor's office, DMV, etc.)
    b. Audio Bibles can be listened to on various devices. You can listen to the *Book of Revelation* in 1 hour and 7 minutes or the book of Philippians in 12 minutes
    c. Bible on computer/internet (there are many varieties)
    d. Pocket electronic Bible—for quick searches or to take and read anywhere you go
    e. Bible(s) on your cell phone.

All the above can be purchased at bookstores or online.

33. **Note:** To assist in studying the Bible, BBG recommends two resources.

    a. A concordance which is a book that aids you in your study of Biblical words or concepts, with an alphabetical listing of words which locates other passages in the Bible with the same word you are studying.

    b. A Bible Dictionary to help you understand words you may not know.

34. Below is a generally accepted timeline of major events/people from the beginning of the Bible's recorded time to the last book of the Bible, for you to use as a reference.

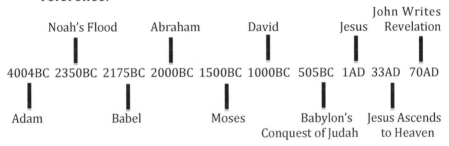

Reminder: Basic Bible Guide is fact based. There are no biased opinions, and it only points out some main parts of each book of the Bible while cross referencing the Old and New Testaments (allowing the Bible to speak for itself). All points and cross references come directly from the Bible and will have the Bible addresses, so you will be able to look them up for yourself.

Additional Reminder: The cross references, below each thinner line and in the corresponding shading (grey and white), are included because even though the Bible is one book, it is very large and covers thousands of years of history, so they are considerably helpful in understanding the entire Bible. They link similar ideas, story lines, and "prophetic" writings, and show when and where these prophesies are fulfilled. Most of them cross from the Old to the New Testament fulfilling or expounding upon what is being read in the Old Testament. All the cross references include the reference of where they are in the Bible, to assist in further study, in this way the Bible teaches itself. Also remember, that in BBG there are no biased teachings or opinions.

Note: Regarding cross references, Jesus said to his followers in Luke 24:44, "These are my words that I spoke to you while I was still with you, that everything written about me in the Law of Moses and the Prophets and the Psalms must be fulfilled."

Day 1

GENESIS OVERVIEW

Title: Genesis is Greek and means "beginning" or "origin".

Author: Thought to be Moses, although there is no verse in Genesis that states Moses is the author. There are several verses such as Exodus 17:14, Exodus 24:4, and Exodus 34:27 (*read these verses another time*), where Moses is recorded as the author of the law which would cover Exodus, Leviticus, Numbers, and Deuteronomy. Therefore, most Jewish and Christian scholars agree that the author of Genesis is Moses.

Audience: There is no specific reference of who this book is written to.

Historical setting: The beginning of Earth's time to Joseph's death in Egypt. Joseph was one of the 12 sons of Jacob-whose name is changed to Israel (Creation Approximately- 4004 B.C.)

Reminder: The first five books of the Old Testament in Hebrew are called the Torah (meaning "law"). In Greek these first five books are called The Pentateuch, or "The Book of the Law of the Lord" given by Moses.

God created *everything*
(Only read these two verses)
Genesis 1:1, 2:1-2

Thoughts and Notes: 4-30-19

God created Universe & Earth - In 7 days?
I like the idea of rest on 7th day

15

Day 2

Someone helped God create the world
Genesis 1:26

52 The Jews said to him, "Now we know that you have a demon! Abraham died, as did the prophets, yet you say, 'If anyone keeps my word, he will never taste death.' 53 Are you greater than our father Abraham, who died? And the prophets died! Who do you make yourself out to be?" 54 Jesus answered, "If I glorify myself, my glory is nothing. It is my Father who glorifies me, of whom you say, 'He is our God.' 55 But you have not known him. I know him. If I were to say that I do not know him, I would be a liar like you, but I do know him and I keep his word. 56 Your father Abraham rejoiced that he would see my day. He saw it and was glad." 57 So the Jews said to him, "You are not yet fifty years old, and have you seen Abraham?" 58 Jesus said to them, "Truly, truly, I say to you, before Abraham was, I am."
John 8:52-58

The first sin/disobedience to God
(only read these 3 verses)

Genesis 2:16-17, 3:6

Note: Sin is an immoral act considered to be a transgression against divine law.

15 Do not love the world or the things in the world. If anyone loves the world, the love of the Father is not in him. 16 For all that is in the world—the desires of the flesh and the desires of the eyes and pride of life—is not from the Father but is from the world.
1 John 2:15-16

Thoughts and Notes:

_____

_____

_____

_____

_____

16

Day 3

Enoch did not die, God took him
Genesis 5:24

---

5 By faith Enoch was taken up so that he should not see death, and he was not found, because God had taken him. Now before he was taken he was commended as having pleased God. 6 And without faith it is impossible to please him, for whoever would draw near to God must believe that he exists and that he rewards those who seek him.

Hebrews 11:5-6

Question for Thought: Why do you think Adam and Eve disobeyed God? (Genesis Chapter 2:16-17, 3:6)

Thoughts and Notes:

_____

_____

_____

_____

_____

_____

_____

_____

_____

_____

_____

Day 4

Mankind grew evil and the Lord wanted to destroy them, but Noah found grace from the Lord
Genesis 6:5-8

God's judgment on Earth and deliverance of Noah
Genesis 7:15-23

18 For Christ also suffered once for sins, the righteous for the unrighteous, that he might bring us to God, being put to death in the flesh but made alive in the spirit, 19 in which he went and proclaimed to the spirits in prison, 20 because they formerly did not obey, when God's patience waited in the days of Noah, while the ark was being prepared, in which a few, that is, eight persons, were brought safely through water.
1 Peter 3:18-20

Thoughts and Notes:

_____

_____

_____

_____

_____

_____

_____

_____

_____

_____

_____

Day 5

The Lord speaks to Abram and he obeys
Genesis 12:1-5

Note: Sarai's name is later changed to Sarah by God, and Abram's name changed to Abraham.

6 just as Abraham "believed God, and it was accounted to him for righteousness." 7 Know then that it is those of faith who are the sons of Abraham. 8 And the Scripture, foreseeing that God would justify the Gentiles by faith, preached the gospel beforehand to Abraham, saying, "In you all the nations shall be blessed." 9 So then, those who are of faith are blessed along with Abraham, the man of faith.
Galatians 3:6-9

Note: Gentiles are people who are not Jewish/Israelites.

Thoughts and Notes:

_____

_____

_____

_____

_____

_____

_____

_____

_____

_____

_____

Day 6

Abram fights, wins, and meets Melchizedek
Genesis 14:17-20

1 For this Melchizedek, king of Salem, priest of the Most High God, met Abraham returning from the slaughter of the kings and blessed him, 2 and to him Abraham apportioned a tenth part of everything. He is first, by translation of his name, king of righteousness, and then he is also king of Salem, that is, king of peace. 3 He is without father or mother or genealogy, having neither beginning of days nor end of life, but resembling the Son of God he continues a priest forever.
Hebrews 7:1-3

God makes a promise to Abram
Genesis 15:2-5

Thoughts and Notes:

_____

_____

_____

_____

_____

_____

_____

_____

_____

_____

_____

_____

Day 7

Abram and his wife attempt to fulfill God's promise on their own
Genesis 16:1-4

Abram becomes Abraham
Genesis 17:5

Thoughts and Notes:

Day 8

Abraham and Sarah have a son, Isaac
Genesis 21:1-4

22 For it is written that Abraham had two sons, one by a slave woman and one by a free woman. 23 But the son of the slave was born according to the flesh, while the son of the free woman was born through promise. 24 Now this may be interpreted allegorically: these women are two covenants. One is from Mount Sinai, bearing children for slavery; she is Hagar. 25 Now Hagar is Mount Sinai in Arabia; she corresponds to the present Jerusalem, for she is in slavery with her children. 26 But the Jerusalem above is free, and she is our mother.
Galatians 4:22-26

General Bible Fact: The word "Bible" means "The Book" (in Greek - "*Ta Biblia*") implying the book of books - superior to other books.

Thoughts and Notes:

_____

_____

_____

_____

_____

_____

_____

_____

_____

_____

Day 9

God tests Abraham
Genesis 22:1-14

20 Do you want to be shown, you foolish person, that faith apart from works is useless? 21 Was not Abraham our father justified by works when he offered up his son Isaac on the altar? 22 You see that faith was active along with his works, and faith was completed by his works; 23 and the Scripture was fulfilled that says, "Abraham believed God, and it was counted to him as righteousness"—and he was called a friend of God.

James 2:20-23

God blesses Isaac
Genesis 25:11

Thoughts and Notes:

_____

_____

_____

_____

_____

_____

_____

_____

_____

_____

Day 10

Isaac and his wife, Rebekah, have twins (Jacob and Esau)
Genesis 25:21-26

Esau sells his birthright to Jacob
Genesis 25:29-33

14 Strive for peace with everyone, and for the holiness without which no one will see the Lord. 15 See to it that no one fails to obtain the grace of God; that no "root of bitterness" springs up and causes trouble, and by it many become defiled; 16 that no one is sexually immoral or unholy like Esau, who sold his birthright for a single meal. 17 For you know that afterward, when he desired to inherit the blessing, he was rejected, for he found no chance to repent, though he sought it with tears.
Hebrews 12:14-17

Thoughts and Notes:

_____

_____

_____

_____

_____

_____

_____

_____

_____

_____

Day 11

Jacob wrestles with God and his name is changed to Israel
Genesis 32:24-28

1 And he told them a parable to the effect that they ought always to pray and not lose heart. 2 He said, "In a certain city there was a judge who neither feared God nor respected man. 3 And there was a widow in that city who kept coming to him and saying, 'Give me justice against my adversary.' 4 For a while he refused, but afterward he said to himself, 'Though I neither fear God nor respect man, 5 yet because this widow keeps bothering me, I will give her justice, so that she will not beat me down by her continual coming.'" 6 And the Lord said, "Hear what the unrighteous judge says. 7 And will not God give justice to his elect, who cry to him day and night? Will he delay long over them? 8 I tell you, he will give justice to them speedily. Nevertheless, when the Son of Man comes, will he find faith on earth?"

Luke 18:1-8

Note: A parable is a short story illustrating a moral lesson or spiritual principle.

God's promise to Jacob
Genesis 35:11-12

Thoughts and Notes:

25

Day 12

Jacob has 12 sons
Genesis 35:23-26

Joseph (Jacob's second youngest son) is sold as a slave to Egypt by his brothers
Genesis 37:28

General Bible Fact: There are 66 separate writings or "books" that make up the Bible. These "books" were given names to identify them, such as Genesis, John and Revelation.

Thoughts and Notes:

_____

_____

_____

_____

_____

_____

_____

_____

_____

_____

_____

_____

_____

Day 13

Joseph becomes second in command of Egypt
Genesis 41:39-40

Joseph forgives his brothers
Genesis 50:15-22

17 Repay no one evil for evil, but give thought to do what is honorable in the sight of all. 18 If possible, so far as it depends on you, live peaceably with all. 19 Beloved, never avenge yourselves, but leave it to the wrath of God, for it is written, "Vengeance is mine, I will repay, says the Lord." 20 To the contrary, "if your enemy is hungry, feed him; if he is thirsty, give him something to drink; for by so doing you will heap burning coals on his head." 21 Do not be overcome by evil, but overcome evil with good.
Romans 12:17-21

Thoughts and Notes:

_____

_____

_____

_____

_____

_____

_____

_____

_____

Day 14

EXODUS OVERVIEW

Title: Exodus in Greek means "exit", "departure", "going out".

Author: Moses

Audience: The Israelites, for their instruction

Reminder: Abraham's son was Isaac, Isaac's son was Jacob, and Jacob's name was changed by God to Israel, and his offspring became the 12 tribes of Israel, or the nation of Israel (the Israelites).

Historical setting: Exodus picks up where Genesis leaves off. 400 years of Israel being slaves to Egypt takes place between Exodus chapters 1 and 2. (This is a cross reference from Acts 7:6 "And God spoke to this effect—that his offspring would be sojourners in a land belonging to others, who would enslave them and afflict them four hundred years."). Exodus ends with the Israelites still journeying on their way to the Promised Land (promised by God to Abraham). (Approximately 1450-1410 B.C.)

Thoughts and Notes:

_____

_____

_____

_____

_____

_____

_____

_____

Day 15

The children of Israel become slaves in Egypt
Exodus 1:8-12

Moses is born and becomes the son of the Pharaoh's daughter
Exodus 2:1-11

Thoughts and Notes:

_____

_____

_____

_____

_____

_____

_____

_____

_____

_____

_____

_____

_____

_____

_____

Day 16

Moses meets the Lord and gets instructions
Exodus 3:2-10

God tells Moses his name
Exodus 3:14-15

2 God spoke to Moses and said to him, "I am the Lord. 3 I appeared to Abraham, to Isaac, and to Jacob, as God Almighty, but by my name the Lord I did not make myself known to them.
Exodus 6:2-3

Thoughts and Notes:

_____

_____

_____

_____

_____

_____

_____

_____

_____

_____

_____

_____

_____

Day 17

Moses makes excuses and hesitates to obey the Lord
Exodus 4:10-15

Moses obeys God and returns to Egypt
Exodus 4:19-20

27 As he said these things, a woman in the crowd raised her voice and said to him, "Blessed is the womb that bore you, and the breasts at which you nursed!" 28 But he said, "Blessed rather are those who hear the word of God and keep it!"
Luke 11:27-28

Thoughts and Notes:

_____

_____

_____

_____

_____

_____

_____

_____

_____

_____

_____

_____

Day 18

The tenth plague on the Egyptians
Exodus 11:4-5

God delivers the Israelites from the tenth plague (an event known as The Passover)
Exodus 12:21-27

24 By faith Moses, when he was grown up, refused to be called the son of Pharaoh's daughter, 25 choosing rather to be mistreated with the people of God than to enjoy the fleeting pleasures of sin. 26 He considered the reproach of Christ greater wealth than the treasures of Egypt, for he was looking to the reward. 27 By faith he left Egypt, not being afraid of the anger of the king, for he endured as seeing him who is invisible. 28 By faith he kept the Passover and sprinkled the blood, so that the Destroyer of the firstborn might not touch them.
Hebrews 11:24-28

Thoughts and Notes:

_____

_____

_____

_____

_____

_____

_____

_____

_____

_____

Day 19

The Israelites escape Egypt and the Lord protects them
Exodus 14:21-31

The LORD provides for the Israelites
Exodus 16:11-15

31 Therefore do not be anxious, saying, 'What shall we eat?' or 'What shall we drink?' or 'What shall we wear?' 32 For the Gentiles seek after all these things, and your heavenly Father knows that you need them all. 33 But seek first the kingdom of God and his righteousness, and all these things will be added to you.
Matthew 6:31-33

Thoughts and Notes:

33

Day 20

God gives the nation of Israel laws, rules, and instructions on how to build the tabernacle
(This passage will take longer than a few minutes to read, read them as time allows)

Note: The Tabernacle was a tent-like structure that God instructed Moses to build. It was to be a place of the physical presence of God to travel with the Israelites. The tabernacle was also where the priest made sacrifices to God to atone for his and the people's sins. It was later replaced by the Temple which was a permanent structure in Jerusalem. The Temple was designed by God who instructed King David on how it should be built. It was later built by David's son King Solomon.
Exodus chapters 20 to 32

Thoughts and Notes:

_____

_____

_____

_____

_____

_____

_____

_____

_____

Day 21

The Israelites create and worship an idol, a false god
Exodus 32:8-9

20 For his invisible attributes, namely, his eternal power and divine nature, have been clearly perceived, ever since the creation of the world, in the things that have been made. So they are without excuse. 21 For although they knew God, they did not honor him as God or give thanks to him, but they became futile in their thinking, and their foolish hearts were darkened. 22 Claiming to be wise, they became fools, 23 and exchanged the glory of the immortal God for images resembling mortal man and birds and animals and creeping things.

24 Therefore God gave them up in the lusts of their hearts to impurity, to the dishonoring of their bodies among themselves, 25 because they exchanged the truth about God for a lie and worshiped and served the creature rather than the Creator, who is blessed forever! Amen.
Romans 1:20-25

Thoughts and Notes:

_____

_____

_____

_____

_____

_____

_____

_____

_____

Day 22

More rules and instructions of how to build the Tabernacle
(This passage will take longer than a few minutes to read, read them as time allows)
Exodus chapters 34 to 40

The tabernacle is completed
(*Only read these 4 verses*)
Exodus 40:17-19, 34

11 But when Christ appeared as a high priest of the good things that have come, then through the greater and more perfect tent (not made with hands, that is, not of this creation) 12 he entered once for all into the holy places, not by means of the blood of goats and calves but by means of his own blood, thus securing an eternal redemption. 13 For if the blood of goats and bulls, and the sprinkling of defiled persons with the ashes of a heifer, sanctify for the purification of the flesh, 14 how much more will the blood of Christ, who through the eternal Spirit offered himself without blemish to God, purify our conscience from dead works to serve the living God.
Hebrews 9:11-14

Thoughts and Notes:

_____

_____

_____

_____

_____

_____

_____

_____

_____

Day 23

LEVITICUS OVERVIEW

Title: Named after the Levites or Levi, (one of the 12 tribes or sons of Israel or Jacob). The Levites were the priests for the nation of Israel, starting with Aaron (Moses's brother) the Levite.

Author: Moses

Audience: The children of Israel or Israelites

Historical setting: The Israelites wandering in the wilderness with Moses and Joshua for 40 years, after the exodus from Egypt. (Approximately 1450-1410 B.C)

Thoughts and Notes:

_____

_____

_____

_____

_____

_____

_____

_____

_____

_____

Day 24

(only read theses 6 verses)
Leviticus 1:3-4, 2:1-2, 3:1-2

1 I appeal to you therefore, brothers, by the mercies of God, to present your bodies as a living sacrifice, holy and acceptable to God, which is your spiritual worship. 2 Do not be conformed to this world, but be transformed by the renewal of your mind, that by testing you may discern what is the will of God, what is good and acceptable and perfect.

Romans 12:1-2

Thoughts and Notes:

_____

_____

_____

_____

_____

_____

_____

_____

_____

_____

_____

_____

_____

Day 25

More offerings for sins
(This passage will take longer than a few minutes to read, read them as time allows)
Leviticus chapters 4 to 8

Aaron's sons (priests) die for not obeying the law
Leviticus 10:1-3

Thoughts and Notes:

_____

_____

_____

_____

_____

_____

_____

_____

_____

_____

_____

_____

_____

_____

_____

Day 26

God gives rules to govern the nation/children of Israel
(This passage will take longer than a few minutes to read, read them as time allows)
Leviticus chapters 11 -16

The priest must sacrifice animals for his sins and those of the people
(only read 3 verses)
Leviticus 16:11, 15, 16

1 My little children, I am writing these things to you so that you may not sin. But if anyone does sin, we have an advocate with the Father, Jesus Christ the righteous. 2 He is the propitiation for our sins, and not for ours only but also for the sins of the whole world.
I John 2:1-2

Thoughts and Notes:

_____

_____

_____

_____

_____

_____

_____

_____

_____

_____

_____

Day 27

These chapters cover other laws, including moral laws
(This passage will take longer than a few minutes to read, read them as time allows)
Leviticus Chapters 17-20

The penalty for particular sins is death
(only read 3 verses)
Leviticus 20:2, 9, 10

20 For when you were slaves of sin, you were free in regard to righteousness. 21 But what fruit were you getting at that time from the things of which you are now ashamed? For the end of those things is death. 22 But now that you have been set free from sin and have become slaves of God, the fruit you get leads to sanctification and its end, eternal life. 23 For the wages of sin is death, but the free gift of God is eternal life in Christ Jesus our Lord.
Romans 6:20-23

Thoughts and Notes:

_____

_____

_____

_____

_____

_____

_____

_____

_____

Day 28

Law of the Sabbath
Leviticus 23:3

10 And a man was there with a withered hand. And they asked him, "Is it lawful to heal on the Sabbath?"—so that they might accuse him. 11 He said to them, "Which one of you who has a sheep, if it falls into a pit on the Sabbath, will not take hold of it and lift it out? 12 Of how much more value is a man than a sheep! So it is lawful to do good on the Sabbath." 13 Then he said to the man, "Stretch out your hand." And the man stretched it out, and it was restored, healthy like the other. 14 But the Pharisees went out and conspired against him, how to destroy him. 15 Jesus, aware of this, withdrew from there. And many followed him, and he healed them all

Matthew 12:10-15

Note: Pharisees were religious leaders of Jesus' time.

Question for Thought: Why would God want the people to rest on the seventh day of the week (Sabbath Day)? (Leviticus 23:3)

Thoughts and Notes:

_____

_____

_____

_____

_____

_____

_____

_____

Day 29

Helping the poor
Leviticus 25:35-37

Reward for obeying the rules/laws
Leviticus 26:3-5

Thoughts and Notes:

_____

_____

_____

_____

_____

_____

_____

_____

_____

_____

_____

_____

_____

_____

_____

Day 30

NUMBERS OVERVIEW

Title: Named from the counting of the people of Israel in chapters 1, 3, and 26 (*do not read these now*).

Author: Thought to be Moses (Numbers 36:13 "These are the commandments and the rules that the LORD commanded through Moses to the people of Israel in the plains of Moab by the Jordan at Jericho.")

Audience: The children of Israel or Israelites

Historical setting: The Israelites still wandering in the wilderness for 40 years after leaving Egypt and before entering the Promised Land (Approximately 1444-1405 B.C.).

A census of the men of Israel
Numbers 1:44-46

Thoughts and Notes:

_____

_____

_____

_____

_____

_____

_____

_____

Day 31

The Levites are counted separately
Numbers 3:39

These chapters cover the priests' (who are Levites) duties and more rules/laws
(Read these chapters another time)
Numbers Chapters 4 - 9

Thoughts and Notes:

_____

_____

_____

_____

_____

_____

_____

_____

_____

_____

_____

_____

_____

_____

_____

_____

_____

Day 32

The Israelites are told to continue to celebrate the Passover
Numbers 9:2-4

Some instructions for the Passover celebration
Numbers 9:12

Note: The Passover is a celebration which was kept in remembrance of the Lord's passing over the houses of the Israelites (Exodus 12:13) when the first born of all the Egyptians were destroyed.

30 When Jesus had received the sour wine, he said, "It is finished," and he bowed his head and gave up his spirit.

31 Since it was the day of Preparation, and so that the bodies would not remain on the cross on the Sabbath (for that Sabbath was a high day), the Jews asked Pilate that their legs might be broken and that they might be taken away. 32 So the soldiers came and broke the legs of the first, and of the otherwho had been crucified with him. 33 But when they came to Jesus and saw that he was already dead, they did not break his legs. 34 But one of the soldiers pierced his side with a spear, and at once there came out blood and water. 35 He who saw it has borne witness—his testimony is true, and he knows that he is telling the truth—that you also may believe. 36 For these things took place that the Scripture might be fulfilled:"Not one of his bones will be broken."
John 19:30-36

Thoughts and Notes:

_____

_____

_____

_____

_____

_____

46

Day 33

The Israelites spy out the "Promised Land"
Numbers 13:1-2

The report of the "Promised Land"
Numbers 13:27-28

Thoughts and Notes:

_____

_____

_____

_____

_____

_____

_____

_____

_____

_____

_____

_____

_____

_____

Day 34

The Israelites were afraid to go to the "Promised Land"
Numbers 14:2-3

4 "I tell you, my friends, do not fear those who kill the body, and after that have nothing more that they can do. 5 But I will warn you whom to fear: fear him who, after he has killed, has authority to cast into hell. Yes, I tell you, fear him! 6 Are not five sparrows sold for two pennies? And not one of them is forgotten before God. 7 Why, even the hairs of your head are all numbered. Fear not; you are of more value than many sparrows.
Luke 12:4-7

Joshua and Caleb trust the Lord
Numbers 14:6-10

Question for Thought: Why do you think the Israelites did not trust God and were afraid to go into the promise land, yet Caleb and Joshua were not? (Numbers 14:6-10)

Thoughts and Notes:

_____

_____

_____

_____

_____

_____

_____

_____

Day 35

Moses prays for the Israelites
Numbers 14:17-24

The consequences for not trusting the Lord and why the Israelites had to wander in the wilderness for 40 years
Numbers 14:29-33

Thoughts and Notes:

Day 36

The priests live off of the tithes
Numbers 18:21-24

Note: A tithe is a requirement in the law of God that requires giving one tenth of your earnings or produce to the storehouse of the Lord (read Leviticus 27:30-33 another time)

9 For it is written in the Law of Moses, "You shall not muzzle an ox when it treads out the grain." Is it for oxen that God is concerned? 10 Does he not certainly speak for our sake? It was written for our sake, because the plowman should plow in hope and the thresher thresh in hope of sharing in the crop. 11 If we have sown spiritual things among you, is it too much if we reap material things from you? 12 If others share this rightful claim on you, do not we even more?

Nevertheless, we have not made use of this right, but we endure anything rather than put an obstacle in the way of the gospel of Christ. 13 Do you not know that those who are employed in the temple service get their food from the temple, and those who serve at the altar share in the sacrificial offerings? 14 In the same way, the Lord commanded that those who proclaim the gospel should get their living by the gospel.

I Corinthians 9:9-14

Thoughts and Notes:

_____

_____

_____

_____

_____

_____

_____

Day 37

Even the Levites tithed
Numbers 18:26

23 "Woe to you, scribes and Pharisees, hypocrites! For you tithe mint and dill and cumin, and have neglected the weightier matters of the law: justice and mercy and faithfulness. These you ought to have done, without neglecting the others.
Matthew 23:23

Thoughts and Notes:

_____

_____

_____

_____

_____

_____

_____

_____

_____

_____

_____

_____

_____

_____

Day 38

Moses and Aaron disobey the Lord
Numbers 20:8-12

1 For I do not want you to be unaware, brothers, that all our fathers were all under the cloud, and all passed through the sea, 2 and all were baptized into Moses in the cloud and in the sea, 3 and all ate the same spiritual food, 4 and all drank the same spiritual drink. For they drank from the spiritual Rock that followed them, and the Rock was Christ. 5 Nevertheless, with most of them God was not pleased, for they were overthrown in the wilderness.

6 Now these things took place as examples for us, that we may not desire evil as they did.
I Corinthians 10:1-6

Thoughts and Notes:

_____

_____

_____

_____

_____

_____

_____

_____

_____

_____

_____

_____

Day 39

Israel complains again; the Lord disciplines them again; Moses prays for them
again, and the Lord delivers them again
Numbers 21:5-9

Note: The symbol of the serpent on the staff, referenced in these passages, is still
used today on the sides of paramedic response vehicles as well as on hospitals.
14 And as Moses lifted up the serpent in the wilderness, so must the Son of Man
be lifted up, 15 that whoever believes in him may have eternal life.

16 "For God so loved the world, that he gave his only Son, that whoever believes
in him should not perish but have eternal life. 17 For God did not send his Son
into the world to condemn the world, but in order that the world might be saved
through him. 18 Whoever believes in him is not condemned, but whoever does
not believe is condemned already, because he has not believed in the name of the
only Son of God.
John 3:14-18

Thoughts and Notes:

Day 40

Balak, king of Moab, sends for the prophet Balaam to curse Israel
Numbers 22:4-7

God tells Balaam, "Do not go"
Numbers 22:12

Thoughts and Notes:

_____

_____

_____

_____

_____

_____

_____

_____

_____

_____

_____

_____

_____

_____

_____

Day 41

Balak offers Balaam more money
Numbers 22:17

Balaam asks God what to do
Numbers 22:19

Thoughts and Notes:

_____

_____

_____

_____

_____

_____

_____

_____

_____

_____

_____

_____

_____

_____

_____

_____

Day 42

God uses an unusual means of communication with Balaam
Numbers 22:27-31

12 But these, like irrational animals, creatures of instinct, born to be caught and destroyed, blaspheming about matters of which they are ignorant, will also be destroyed in their destruction, 13 suffering wrong as the wage for their wrongdoing. They count it pleasure to revel in the daytime. They are blots and blemishes, reveling in their deceptions, while they feast with you. 14 They have eyes full of adultery, insatiable for sin. They entice unsteady souls. They have hearts trained in greed. Accursed children! 15 Forsaking the right way, they have gone astray. They have followed the way of Balaam, the son of Beor, who loved gain from wrongdoing, 16 but was rebuked for his own transgression; a speechless donkey spoke with human voice and restrained the prophet's madness.

17 These are waterless springs and mists driven by a storm. For them the gloom of utter darkness has been reserved.
II Peter 2:12-17

Thoughts and Notes:

_____

_____

_____

_____

_____

_____

_____

_____

Day 43

The Lord chose Joshua to be Israel's next leader
Numbers 27:22-23

Making a vow
Numbers 30:2

33 "Again you have heard that it was said to those of old, 'You shall not swear falsely, but shall perform to the Lord what you have sworn.' 34 But I say to you, Do not take an oath at all, either by heaven, for it is the throne of God, 35 or by the earth, for it is his footstool, or by Jerusalem, for it is the city of the great King. 36 And do not take an oath by your head, for you cannot make one hair white or black. 37 Let what you say be simply 'Yes' or 'No'; anything more than this comes from evil.
Matthew 5:33-37

Thoughts and Notes:

Day 44

DEUTERONOMY OVERVIEW

Title: Named after the Greek word *Deuteronomion* meaning *"second law giving"* (the first being Exodus and Leviticus).

Author: Thought to be Moses

Audience: The children of Israel or Israelites

Historical setting: The last days of wandering in the wilderness, before entering the Promised Land, until Moses' death. (Approximately 1406-1220 B.C)

Thoughts and Notes:

_____

_____

_____

_____

_____

_____

_____

_____

_____

_____

_____

_____

_____

Day 45

The Israelites begin to take possession of the "Promised Land"
Deuteronomy 2:24

Moses reminds the Israelites not to forget God's Laws
Deuteronomy 4:1

10 Therefore, brothers, be all the more diligent to confirm your calling and election, for if you practice these qualities you will never fall. 11 For in this way there will be richly provided for you an entrance into the eternal kingdom of our Lord and Savior Jesus Christ.
II Peter 1:10, 11

Thoughts and Notes:

Day 46

36 "Teacher, which is the great commandment in the Law?" 37 And he said to him, "You shall love the Lord your God with all your heart and with all your soul and with all your mind. 38 This is the great and first commandment. 39 And a second is like it: You shall love your neighbor as yourself. 40 On these two commandments depend all the Law and the Prophets."
Matthew 22:36-40

Question for Thought: We learn the most important commandment in Deuteronomy, why do you think it is the most important? (Deuteronomy 6:4-6)

Thoughts and Notes:

_____

_____

_____

_____

_____

_____

_____

_____

_____

_____

_____

Day 47

Israel is God's holy chosen people
Deuteronomy 7:6-8

34 So Peter opened his mouth and said: "Truly I understand that God shows no partiality, 35 but in every nation anyone who fears him and does what is right is acceptable to him. 36 As for the word that he sent to Israel, preaching good news of peace through Jesus Christ (he is Lord of all), 37 you yourselves know what happened throughout all Judea, beginning from Galilee after the baptism that John proclaimed: 38 how God anointed Jesus of Nazareth with the Holy Spirit and with power. He went about doing good and healing all who were oppressed by the devil, for God was with him. 39 And we are witnesses of all that he did both in the country of the Jews and in Jerusalem. They put him to death by hanging him on a tree, 40 but God raised him on the third day and made him to appear, 41 not to all the people but to us who had been chosen by God as witnesses, who ate and drank with him after he rose from the dead. 42 And he commanded us to preach to the people and to testify that he is the one appointed by God to be judge of the living and the dead. 43 To him all the prophets bear witness that everyone who believes in him receives forgiveness of sins through his name."
Acts 10:34-43

Note: The Holy Spirit is the spirit of God which is his promise that he gives to believers of Jesus as proof of His forgiveness and their salvation.

The Lord warns Israel not to follow the practices of the people in the Land
Deuteronomy 12:29-31

Thoughts and Notes:

Day 48

God's warning against false prophets
Deuteronomy 13:1-3

24 For false christs and false prophets will arise and perform great signs and wonders, so as to lead astray, if possible, even the elect. 25 See, I have told you beforehand. 26 So, if they say to you, 'Look, he is in the wilderness,' do not go out. If they say, 'Look, he is in the inner rooms,' do not believe it. 27 For as the lightning comes from the east and shines as far as the west, so will be the coming of the Son of Man. 28 Wherever the corpse is, there the vultures will gather.
Matthew 24:24-28

The Passover is reviewed
Deuteronomy 16:5-6

12 So Jesus also suffered outside the gate in order to sanctify the people through his own blood. 13 Therefore let us go to him outside the camp and bear the reproach he endured. 14 For here we have no lasting city, but we seek the city that is to come. 15 Through him then let us continually offer up a sacrifice of praise to God, that is, the fruit of lips that acknowledge his name.
Hebrews 13:12-15

Thoughts and Notes:

_____

_____

_____

_____

_____

_____

_____

_____

Day 49

God has rules concerning cleanliness
Deuteronomy 23:12, 13

21 Therefore put away all filthiness and rampant wickedness and receive with meekness the implanted word, which is able to save your souls.
James 1:21

The law is written in stone
Deuteronomy 27:2-3

11 For God shows no partiality.

12 For all who have sinned without the law will also perish without the law, and all who have sinned under the law will be judged by the law. 13 For it is not the hearers of the law who are righteous before God, but the doers of the law who will be justified. 14 For when Gentiles, who do not have the law, by nature do what the law requires, they are a law to themselves, even though they do not have the law. 15 They show that the work of the law is written on their hearts, while their conscience also bears witness, and their conflicting thoughts accuse or even excuse them 16 on that day when, according to my gospel, God judges the secrets of men by Christ Jesus.
Romans 2:11-16

Thoughts and Notes:

Day 50

Moses encourages the people and Joshua
Deuteronomy 31:6-8

5 Keep your life free from love of money, and be content with what you have, for he has said, "I will never leave you nor forsake you." 6 So we can confidently say,

"The Lord is my helper;
I will not fear;
what can man do to me?"
Hebrews 13:5-6

Thoughts and Notes:

_____

_____

_____

_____

_____

_____

_____

_____

_____

_____

_____

_____

_____

Day 51

The final song of Moses
Deuteronomy 32:43-47

Moses gets to see the Promised Land
Deuteronomy 34:1-5

29 And as he was praying, the appearance of his face was altered, and his clothing became dazzling white. 30 And behold, two men were talking with him, Moses and Elijah, 31 who appeared in glory and spoke of his departure, which he was about to accomplish at Jerusalem.
Luke 9:29-31

Thoughts and Notes:

65

Day 52

JOSHUA OVERVIEW

Title: Named after Joshua who led Israel to the Promised Land, after Moses died

Author: Probably Joshua (Joshua 24:26 "And Joshua wrote these words in the Book of the Law of God. And he took a large stone and set it up there under the terebinth that was by the sanctuary of the LORD.")

Audience: This is a historical book with no specific audience.

Historical setting: The end of 40 years of wandering and taking possession of the Promised Land, promised by God to Abraham; Abraham's son Isaac; Isaac's son Jacob, and Moses. (Approximately 1404-1390 B.C.)

Reminder: The next 12 books of the Old Testament are recognized as "Historical Books", recording the history of the Israelites from the time of the possession of their "inheritance" from God through their many kings, until their destruction and captivity to Babylon (the Babylonians).

Thoughts and Notes:

_____

_____

_____

_____

_____

_____

_____

_____

Day 53

The Lord speaks to Joshua
Joshua 1:1-2

Rahab helps two Israelite spies
Joshua 2:3-6

Thoughts and Notes:

_____

_____

_____

_____

_____

_____

_____

_____

_____

_____

_____

_____

_____

_____

Day 54

Israel crosses the Jordan River
Joshua 3:13-17

Israel defeats Jericho, and spares Rahab
Joshua 6:20-25

30 By faith the walls of Jericho fell down after they had been encircled for seven days. 31 By faith Rahab the prostitute did not perish with those who were disobedient, because she had given a friendly welcome to the spies.
Hebrews 11:30-31

Thoughts and Notes:

_____

_____

_____

_____

_____

_____

_____

_____

_____

_____

_____

_____

_____

Day 55

Ai defeats Israel
Joshua 7:3-5

Why Ai defeated Israel
Joshua 7:20-21

Joshua prays and stops the sun
Joshua 10:12-14

Thoughts and Notes:

_____

_____

_____

_____

_____

_____

_____

_____

_____

_____

_____

_____

_____

Day 56

What happened to Balaam (the man the donkey spoke to)
Joshua 13:22

Caleb gets his own land
Joshua 14:13-14

Thoughts and Notes:

_____

_____

_____

_____

_____

_____

_____

_____

_____

_____

_____

Day 57

The Lord's promise is fulfilled
Joshua 21:44-45

Joshua's final instructions to Israel
Joshua 23:6-8

5 And the devil took him up and showed him all the kingdoms of the world in a moment of time, 6 and said to him, "To you I will give all this authority and their glory, for it has been delivered to me, and I give it to whom I will. 7 If you, then, will worship me, it will all be yours." 8 And Jesus answered him, "It is written,

"'You shall worship the Lord your God,
  and him only shall you serve.'"
Luke 4:5-8

Thoughts and Notes:

Day 58

Joshua says to choose whom to serve
Joshua 24:15

Joshua dies
Joshua 24:25-29

25 Jesus said to her, "I am the resurrection and the life. Whoever believes in me, though he die, yet shall he live,
John 11:25

Question for Thought: What are the things we choose to serve today? (Joshua 24:15)

Thoughts and Notes:

_____

_____

_____

_____

_____

_____

_____

_____

_____

_____

_____

Day 59

JUDGES OVERVIEW

Title: Named after the "Judges" who were Israel's leaders (Judges 2:16-18 "Then the LORD raised up judges, who saved them out of the hand of those who plundered them. [17] Yet they did not listen to their judges, for they whored after other gods and bowed down to them. They soon turned aside from the way in which their fathers had walked, who had obeyed the commandments of the LORD, and they did not do so. [18] Whenever the LORD raised up judges for them, the LORD was with the judge, and he saved them from the hand of their enemies all the days of the judge. For the LORD was moved to pity by their groaning because of those who afflicted and oppressed them.")

Author: There is no reference as to who the author is.

Audience: This is a historical book with no specific reference.

Historical setting: Israel's first 350 years as a nation in its own land, after the death of Joshua, before there were kings in Israel. (Approximately 1450-1300 B.C.)

Israel did not drive out all the land's inhabitants
Judges 1:28

Thoughts and Notes:

Day 60

Israel disobeys the LORD
Judges 2:1-4

46 "Why do you call me 'Lord, Lord,' and not do what I tell you? 47 Everyone who comes to me and hears my words and does them, I will show you what he is like: 48 he is like a man building a house, who dug deep and laid the foundation on the rock. And when a flood arose, the stream broke against that house and could not shake it, because it had been well built. 49 But the one who hears and does not do them is like a man who built a house on the ground without a foundation. When the stream broke against it, immediately it fell, and the ruin of that house was great."

Luke 6:46-49

Thoughts and Notes:

_____

_____

_____

_____

_____

_____

_____

_____

_____

_____

_____

_____

Day 61

Israel is unfaithful again and gets disciplined
Judges 4:1-2

11 My son, do not despise the Lord's discipline
   or be weary of his reproof,
12 for the Lord reproves him whom he loves,
   as a father the son in whom he delights.

13 Blessed is the one who finds wisdom,
   and the one who gets understanding,
Proverbs 3:11-13

Thoughts and Notes:

_____

_____

_____

_____

_____

_____

_____

_____

_____

_____

_____

_____

Day 62

Israel cries out to the Lord
Judges 4:3

God uses a woman prophetess and judge
Judges 4:4

Thoughts and Notes:

_____

_____

_____

_____

_____

_____

_____

_____

_____

_____

_____

_____

_____

_____

_____

Day 63

God delivers Israel
Judges 4:15

God uses 300 men to defeat 120,000 men
Judges 8:4-12

Thoughts and Notes:

_____

_____

_____

_____

_____

_____

_____

_____

_____

_____

_____

_____

_____

_____

Day 64

Israel sins again
Judges 13:1

God rescues them again through Samson
Judges 16:27-30

Israel has no king
Judges 21:25

Question for Thought: What do you make of Israel sinning over and over again and God rescuing them over and over again? (Judges 13:1 and Judges 16:27-30)

Thoughts and Notes:

_____

_____

_____

_____

_____

_____

_____

_____

_____

_____

_____

Day 65

RUTH OVERVIEW

Title: Named after the main individual of this book, a widowed woman who moved from Moab to Israel with her mother-in-law, Naomi.

Author: There is no reference in this book as to the author.

Audience: This is a historical book with no specific reference.

Historical setting: During the days of Judges in Israel. (Approximately 1010-1150 B.C.)

Ruth loved and respected her mother-in-law, Naomi
Ruth 1:14-17

Thoughts and Notes:

_____

_____

_____

_____

_____

_____

_____

_____

Day 66

Boaz was compassionate to Ruth because of her kindness to Naomi
Ruth 2:8-12

Boaz marries Ruth
Ruth 4:13-14

Thoughts and Notes:

_____

_____

_____

_____

_____

_____

_____

_____

_____

_____

_____

_____

_____

_____

_____

Day 67

Boaz and Ruth are King David's (the future king of Israel) great-grandparents
Ruth 4:17

5 and Salmon the father of Boaz by Rahab, and Boaz the father of Obed by Ruth, and Obed the father of Jesse, 6 and Jesse the father of David the king. And David was the father of Solomon by the wife of Uriah.
Matthew 1:5-6

Note: You will read about the people, mentioned in the above verse, later in this study.

Thoughts and Notes:

_____

_____

_____

_____

_____

_____

_____

_____

_____

_____

_____

_____

Day 68

I SAMUEL OVERVIEW

Title: I Samuel and II Samuel were named after Samuel, the Prophet and Judge of Israel.

Reminder: Prophets are people who convey messages to others, as they have been revealed to them by God (usually concerning the future).

Author: There is no reference as to the author.

Audience: This is a historical book with no specific reference.

Historical setting: Samuel was Israel's last Judge, who also chose the first king of Israel, named Saul, until the death of Saul. (Approximately 1043-1011 B.C.)

Hannah prays to have a son
I Samuel 1:8-11

Thoughts and Notes:

_____

_____

_____

_____

_____

_____

_____

Day 69

Hannah's prayer is answered
I Samuel 1:20

Hannah honors her prayer
I Samuel 1:28

Thoughts and Notes:

_____

_____

_____

_____

_____

_____

_____

_____

_____

_____

_____

_____

_____

_____

_____

Day 70

Eli, the Priest, had corrupt sons
I Samuel 2:12

God's judgment on Eli and his sons
I Samuel 4:17-18

Thoughts and Notes:

_____

_____

_____

_____

_____

_____

_____

_____

_____

_____

_____

_____

_____

_____

Day 71

Samuel is Israel's judge and gives them advice
I Samuel 7:3-4

38 And Peter said to them, "Repent and be baptized every one of you in the name of Jesus Christ for the forgiveness of your sins, and you will receive the gift of the Holy Spirit. 39 For the promise is for you and for your children and for all who are far off, everyone whom the Lord our God calls to himself."
Acts 2:38-39

Israel asks for a king
I Samuel 8:4-7

Thoughts and Notes:

_____

_____

_____

_____

_____

_____

_____

_____

_____

_____

_____

_____

_____

Day 72

Saul is the first king of Israel
I Samuel 10:21-24

King Saul broke the Lord's commandment
I Samuel 13:11-14

Question for Thought: Why would Israel ask for a king when God was their leader? (I Samuel 8:4-7)

Thoughts and Notes:

_____

_____

_____

_____

_____

_____

_____

_____

_____

_____

_____

_____

_____

_____

Day 73

How the Lord sees people
I Samuel 16:7

27 "Woe to you, scribes and Pharisees, hypocrites! For you are like whitewashed tombs, which outwardly appear beautiful, but within are full of dead people's bones and all uncleanness. 28 So you also outwardly appear righteous to others, but within you are full of hypocrisy and lawlessness.
Matthew 23:27-28

David is anointed king and the Lord's spirit departs from King Saul
I Samuel 16:13-14

Thoughts and Notes:

_____

_____

_____

_____

_____

_____

_____

_____

_____

_____

_____

_____

_____

Day 74

David kills the Giant, Goliath
I Samuel 17:45-50

12 For we do not wrestle against flesh and blood, but against the rulers, against the authorities, against the cosmic powers over this present darkness, against the spiritual forces of evil in the heavenly places. 13 Therefore take up the whole armor of God, that you may be able to withstand in the evil day, and having done all, to stand firm. 14 Stand therefore, having fastened on the belt of truth, and having put on the breastplate of righteousness, 15 and, as shoes for your feet, having put on the readiness given by the gospel of peace. 16 In all circumstances take up the shield of faith, with which you can extinguish all the flaming darts of the evil one; 17 and take the helmet of salvation, and the sword of the Spirit, which is the word of God,
Ephesians 6:12-17

Thoughts and Notes:

_____

_____

_____

_____

_____

_____

_____

_____

_____

_____

Day 75

King Saul chases David, but David spares Saul
I Samuel 24:3-12

19 Beloved, never avenge yourselves, but leave it to the wrath of God, for it is written, "Vengeance is mine, I will repay, says the Lord."
Romans 12:19

King Saul and his sons die
I Samuel 31:2-6

Thoughts and Notes:

_____

_____

_____

_____

_____

_____

_____

_____

_____

_____

_____

_____

_____

Day 76

II SAMUEL OVERVIEW

Title: I Samuel and II Samuel were named after Samuel, the Prophet and Judge of Israel.

Author: There is no reference about who wrote it.

Audience: This is a historical book with no specific reference.

Historical setting: This book covers the period after the death of King Saul (Israel's first king) to when King David (Israel's second king) was close to his death. (Approximately 1011-1004 B.C.)

David becomes king of Israel
II Samuel 5:3

Thoughts and Notes:

_____

_____

_____

_____

_____

_____

_____

_____

_____

Day 77

King David takes Jerusalem as his home
II Samuel 5:6-7

The ark of the Lord (a gold plated case, containing important relics of God) is brought to Jerusalem
(Read Exodus 25:10-16 and Hebrews 9:4 as time allows)
II Samuel 6:14-15

Thoughts and Notes:

_____

_____

_____

_____

_____

_____

_____

_____

_____

_____

_____

_____

_____

_____

_____

Day 78

II Samuel 7:12-15

31 And behold, you will conceive in your womb and bear a son, and you shall call his name Jesus. 32 He will be great and will be called the Son of the Most High. And the Lord God will give to him the throne of his father David, 33 and he will reign over the house of Jacob forever, and of his kingdom there will be no end."
Luke 1:31-33

Thoughts and Notes:

_____

_____

_____

_____

_____

_____

_____

_____

_____

_____

_____

_____

_____

_____

Day 79

King David sins
II Samuel 11:2-5

King David has Bathsheba's husband killed
II Samuel 11:15-17

Thoughts and Notes:

_____

_____

_____

_____

_____

_____

_____

_____

_____

_____

_____

_____

_____

_____

_____

_____

Day 80

King David marries Bathsheba
II Samuel 11:26-27

The prophet Nathan confronts King David's sin
II Samuel 12:9

Thoughts and Notes:

_____
_____
_____
_____
_____
_____
_____
_____
_____
_____
_____
_____
_____
_____
_____
_____

Day 81

King David's response to Nathan
II Samuel 12:13

8 If we say we have no sin, we deceive ourselves, and the truth is not in us. 9 If we confess our sins, he is faithful and just to forgive us our sins and to cleanse us from all unrighteousness. 10 If we say we have not sinned, we make him a liar, and his word is not in us.

King David and Queen Bathsheba's baby dies
II Samuel 12:22-23

Question for Thought: How is David a "man after God's own heart" when he was capable of adultery and essentially murder? (II Samuel 11:15-17 and II Samuel 12:13)

Thoughts and Notes:

_____

_____

_____

_____

_____

_____

_____

_____

_____

_____

Day 82

King David and Queen Bathsheba have another son, Solomon
II Samuel 12:24

King David sings thanks and praise to the Lord
II Samuel 22:1-4

16 Rejoice always, 17 pray without ceasing, 18 give thanks in all circumstances; for this is the will of God in Christ Jesus for you.
I Thessalonians 5:16-18

Thoughts and Notes:

_____

_____

_____

_____

_____

_____

_____

_____

_____

_____

_____

_____

_____

_____

Day 83

I KINGS OVERVIEW

Title: I Kings and II Kings are named after the chronicles, or archives, of the many kings of Israel and Judah that these books cover.

Author: Unknown, no reference in this book as to the author.

Audience: This is a historical book with no specific audience.

Historical setting: This book includes the last days of David (King of Israel) through Israel being divided into two kingdoms (Israel and Judah), and ends with Jehoram being king of Judah, and Ahaziah (king Ahab's son) being king of Israel (Approximately 600-330 B.C.)

Note: Jerusalem was the capital of Judah, and Samaria was the capital of Israel.

King David chooses Solomon to be the next king
I Kings 1:29-30

Thoughts and Notes:

_____

_____

_____

_____

_____

_____

Day 84

King David's final instructions to Solomon
I Kings 2:1-4

King David dies and Solomon replaces him as king
I Kings 2:10-12

Thoughts and Notes:

_____

_____

_____

_____

_____

_____

_____

_____

_____

_____

_____

_____

_____

_____

_____

_____

Day 85

King Solomon's request to God
I Kings 3:9

5 If any of you lacks wisdom, let him ask God, who gives generously to all without reproach, and it will be given him. 6 But let him ask in faith, with no doubting, for the one who doubts is like a wave of the sea that is driven and tossed by the wind. 7 For that person must not suppose that he will receive anything from the Lord; 8 he is a double-minded man, unstable in all his ways.
James 1:5-8

King Solomon starts to build the Temple for the Lord
I Kings 6:1

Reminder: The Temple replaced the Tabernacle as a permanent structure in Jerusalem. The Temple was to be a place of the physical presence of God, as well as a place for the priests to make sacrifices to atone for their's and the people's sins.

Thoughts and Notes:

Day 86

King Solomon prays for God's presence to be in the Temple
I Kings 8:26-29

18 Flee from sexual immorality. Every other sin a person commits is outside the body, but the sexually immoral person sins against his own body. 19 Or do you not know that your body is a temple of the Holy Spirit within you, whom you have from God? You are not your own, 20 for you were bought with a price. So glorify God in your body.
I Corinthians 6:18-20

The queen of Sheba visits Solomon
I Kings 10:1-3

Thoughts and Notes:

_____

_____

_____

_____

_____

_____

_____

_____

_____

_____

_____

Day 87

King Solomon sins
I Kings 11:1-6

King Solomon's consequences
I Kings 11:31-32

7 Do not be deceived: God is not mocked, for whatever one sows, that will he also reap. 8 For the one who sows to his own flesh will from the flesh reap corruption, but the one who sows to the Spirit will from the Spirit reap eternal life.
Galatians 6:7-8

Thoughts and Notes:

_____

_____

_____

_____

_____

_____

_____

_____

_____

_____

_____

_____

_____

Day 88

King Solomon dies and Rehoboam becomes King of Israel
I Kings 11:42-43

The Kingdom of Israel is divided
I Kings 12:18-24

Thoughts and Notes:

_____

_____

_____

_____

_____

_____

_____

_____

_____

_____

_____

_____

_____

_____

_____

_____

2013 Basic Bible Guide

Day 89

Ahab is a wicked king
I Kings 16:33

Elijah the prophet confronts King Ahab
I Kings 17:1

Thoughts and Notes:

_____

_____

_____

_____

_____

_____

_____

_____

_____

_____

_____

_____

_____

Day 90

Elijah meets and confronts King Ahab again
I Kings 18:17-18

Elijah's victory for God
I Kings 18:22-39

Thoughts and Notes:

_____

_____

_____

_____

_____

_____

_____

_____

_____

_____

_____

_____

_____

_____

_____

Day 91

Queen Jezebel (King Ahab's wife) threatens Elijah, and he flees
I Kings 19:1-5

God's revelation to Elijah
I Kings 19:11-18

Thoughts and Notes:

_____

_____

_____

_____

_____

_____

_____

_____

_____

_____

_____

_____

_____

_____

Day 92

King Ahab fasts and the Lord relents
I Kings 21:27-29

4 You adulterous people! Do you not know that friendship with the world is enmity with God? Therefore whoever wishes to be a friend of the world makes himself an enemy of God. 5 Or do you suppose it is to no purpose that the Scripture says, "He yearns jealously over the spirit that he has made to dwell in us"? 6 But he gives more grace. Therefore it says, "God opposes the proud, but gives grace to the humble." 7 Submit yourselves therefore to God. Resist the devil, and he will flee from you. 8 Draw near to God, and he will draw near to you. Cleanse your hands, you sinners, and purify your hearts, you double-minded. 9 Be wretched and mourn and weep. Let your laughter be turned to mourning and your joy to gloom. 10 Humble yourselves before the Lord, and he will exalt you.
James 4:4-10

Thoughts and Notes:

_____

_____

_____

_____

_____

_____

_____

_____

_____

Day 93

II KINGS OVERVIEW

Title: I Kings and II Kings are named after the chronicles, or archives, of the many kings of Israel and Judah that these books cover.

Author: Unknown, no reference in this book as to the author.

Audience: This is a historical book with no specific audience.

Historical setting: II Kings picks up right where I Kings leaves off and ends with the conquest of Israel and Judah. (Approximately 600-330 B.C.)

Note: Israel is conquered by Assyria, and Judah is conquered by Babylon.

The prophet Elijah and his servant Elisha
II Kings 2:8-14

Thoughts and Notes:

_____

_____

_____

_____

_____

_____

_____

_____

Day 94

One of Elisha's miracles
II Kings 4:32-35

Another of Elisha's miracles
II Kings 6:5-7

Thoughts and Notes:

_____

_____

_____

_____

_____

_____

_____

_____

_____

_____

_____

_____

_____

_____

Day 95

Queen Jezebel, the wife of King Ahab, dies
II Kings 9:30-37

35 Heaven and earth will pass away, but my words will not pass away.
Matthew 24:35

Thoughts and Notes:

_____

_____

_____

_____

_____

_____

_____

_____

_____

_____

_____

_____

_____

_____

_____

Day 96

God has compassion on Israel
II Kings 13:22-23

35 And Jesus went throughout all the cities and villages, teaching in their synagogues and proclaiming the gospel of the kingdom and healing every disease and every affliction. 36 When he saw the crowds, he had compassion for them, because they were harassed and helpless, like sheep without a shepherd.

There were many kings in Israel and Judah
(read these verses another time)
II Kings 14:1, 15:1, 15:8, 15:17, 16:1, 17:1, 18:1

Thoughts and Notes:

_____

_____

_____

_____

_____

_____

_____

_____

_____

_____

_____

_____

Day 97

King Hezekiah prays for the Lord's help
II Kings 19:14-16

An Angel of the Lord rescues Judah
II Kings 19:35-37

Thoughts and Notes:

_____

_____

_____

_____

_____

_____

_____

_____

_____

_____

_____

_____

_____

_____

Day 98

Josiah, king of Judah, was faithful to God
II Kings 23:24-25

1 Therefore, since we are surrounded by so great a cloud of witnesses, let us also lay aside every weight, and sin which clings so closely, and let us run with endurance the race that is set before us, 2 looking to Jesus, the founder and perfecter of our faith, who for the joy that was set before him endured the cross, despising the shame, and is seated at the right hand of the throne of God.
Hebrews 12:1-2

Judah falls to Babylon and Jerusalem is destroyed
II Kings 25:8-15

Thoughts and Notes:

_____

_____

_____

_____

_____

_____

_____

_____

_____

_____

_____

Day 99

I CHRONICLES OVERVIEW

Title: In Hebrew Chronicles means "accounts of the days".

Author: There is no author mentioned.

Audience: This is a historical book with no specific audience.

Historical setting: I & II Chronicles cover the same time period as I and II Kings; with I Chronicles ending with the death of King David (Approximately 450 - 410 B.C.)

A detailed lineage of Israel starting with Adam, the first man
(*read these chapters another time*)
I Chronicles Chapters 1 - 9

Thoughts and Notes:

_____

_____

_____

_____

_____

_____

_____

_____

_____

Day 100

Musicians of King David
I Chronicles 6:31-32

17 Therefore do not be foolish, but understand what the will of the Lord is. 18 And do not get drunk with wine, for that is debauchery, but be filled with the Spirit, 19 addressing one another in psalms and hymns and spiritual songs, singing and making melody to the Lord with your heart, 20 giving thanks always and for everything to God the Father in the name of our Lord Jesus Christ,
Ephesians 5:17-20

Thoughts and Notes:

_____

_____

_____

_____

_____

_____

_____

_____

_____

_____

_____

_____

_____

Day 101

King David asks God if he should go to battle
I Chronicles 14:10

1 What causes quarrels and what causes fights among you? Is it not this, that your passions are at war within you? 2 You desire and do not have, so you murder. You covet and cannot obtain, so you fight and quarrel. You do not have, because you do not ask. 3 You ask and do not receive, because you ask wrongly, to spend it on your passions. 4 You adulterous people! Do you not know that friendship with the world is enmity with God? Therefore whoever wishes to be a friend of the world makes himself an enemy of God. 5 Or do you suppose it is to no purpose that the Scripture says, "He yearns jealously over the spirit that he has made to dwell in us"? 6 But he gives more grace. Therefore it says, "God opposes the proud, but gives grace to the humble."
James 4:1-6

Thoughts and Notes:

_____

_____

_____

_____

_____

_____

_____

_____

_____

_____

Day 102

Ministry to the Lord
(*only read these 3 versus*)
I Chronicles 16:37, 16:41-42

23 But the hour is coming, and is now here, when the true worshipers will worship the Father in spirit and truth, for the Father is seeking such people to worship him. 24 God is spirit, and those who worship him must worship in spirit and truth."

John 4:23-24

Thoughts and Notes:

_____

_____

_____

_____

_____

_____

_____

_____

_____

_____

_____

_____

_____

_____

_____

Day 103

King David's administration
I Chronicles 18:14-17

17 Moses' father-in-law said to him, "What you are doing is not good. 18 You and the people with you will certainly wear yourselves out, for the thing is too heavy for you. You are not able to do it alone. 19 Now obey my voice; I will give you advice, and God be with you! You shall represent the people before God and bring their cases to God, 20 and you shall warn them about the statutes and the laws, and make them know the way in which they must walk and what they must do. 21 Moreover, look for able men from all the people, men who fear God, who are trustworthy and hate a bribe, and place such men over the people as chiefs of thousands, of hundreds, of fifties, and of tens. 22 And let them judge the people at all times. Every great matter they shall bring to you, but any small matter they shall decide themselves. So it will be easier for you, and they will bear the burden with you.
Exodus 18:17-22

Thoughts and Notes:

_____

_____

_____

_____

_____

_____

_____

_____

_____

Day 104

King David makes the plans for the house/Temple of God for Solomon to build
I Chronicles 22:5

Note: The temple was a permanent structure built in Jerusalem, for the presence of God to dwell in with his people, the Israelites.

The people willingly gave to build God's temple
I Chronicles 29:6-9

6 The point is this: whoever sows sparingly will also reap sparingly, and whoever sows bountifully will also reap bountifully. 7 Each one must give as he has decided in his heart, not reluctantly or under compulsion, for God loves a cheerful giver.
II Corinthians 9:6-7

Thoughts and Notes:

_____

_____

_____

_____

_____

_____

_____

_____

_____

_____

_____

118

Day 105

II CHRONICLES OVERVIEW

Title: In Hebrew Chronicles means "accounts of the days".

Author: There is no author mentioned.

Audience: This is a historical book with no specific audience.

Historical setting: Starts with Solomon (David's son) becoming king of Israel and ends the same as II Kings, with the destruction of Israel and Judah. (Approximately 971 - 561 B.C.)

Note: The kingdom of Israel was split in two when Rehoboam (Solomon's son) was king of Israel. Jeroboam became the first king of Israel after the split, while Rehoboam remained king of Judah.

King Solomon Builds a magnificent Temple for the Lord
II Chronicles 3:4-8

Note: A Cherubim is a celestial being used by God for several purposes in the Hebrew Bible.

Thoughts and Notes:

_____

_____

_____

_____

_____

_____

Day 106

King Solomon prays after the Temple is complete
II Chronicles 6:13-15

6 And without faith it is impossible to please him, for whoever would draw near to God must believe that he exists and that he rewards those who seek him.
Hebrews 11:6

King Solomon was extremely wealthy
II Chronicles 9:13-14

34 And calling the crowd to him with his disciples, he said to them, "If anyone would come after me, let him deny himself and take up his cross and follow me. 35 For whoever would save his life will lose it, but whoever loses his life for my sake and the gospel's will save it. 36 For what does it profit a man to gain the whole world and forfeit his soul? 37 For what can a man give in return for his soul?
Mark 8:34-37

Thoughts and Notes:

_____

_____

_____

_____

_____

_____

_____

_____

_____

Day 107

Uzziah was a good king of Judah
II Chronicles 26:3-5

King Uzziah's sin
II Chronicles 26:16-18

Thoughts and Notes:

_____

_____

_____

_____

_____

_____

_____

_____

_____

_____

_____

_____

_____

Day 108

18 Pride goes before destruction,
And a haughty spirit before a fall.
Proverbs 16:18

Question for Thought: Do you think that being prideful still has consequences today, as it did for King Uzziah? (II Chronicles 26:19-21)

Thoughts and Notes:

_____

_____

_____

_____

_____

_____

_____

_____

_____

_____

_____

_____

Day 109

The book of the law is found
II Chronicles 34:15

23 since you have been born again, not of perishable seed but of imperishable, through the living and abiding word of God; 24 for
"All flesh is like grass
and all its glory like the flower of grass.
The grass withers,
and the flower falls,
25 but the word of the Lord remains forever."

And this word is the good news that was preached to you.
I Peter 1:23-25

Jerusalem falls to Babylon
II Chronicles 36:20-21

Thoughts and Notes:

_____

_____

_____

_____

_____

_____

_____

_____

Day 110

EZRA OVERVIEW

Title: Named after the main character of this book. Ezra was a descendant of Aaron (Moses' brother - the first priest).

Author: Most likely Ezra, but there is no specific reference.

Audience: This is a historical book with no specific audience.

Historical setting: After the fall of Jerusalem to Babylon some of the Israelites were taken into captivity for 70 years (Ezra 2:1 "Now these were the people of the province who came up out of the captivity of those exiles whom Nebuchadnezzar the king of Babylon had carried captive to Babylonia. They returned to Jerusalem and Judah, each to his own town."). Ezra was released from captivity by the world power of that time (Persia) to return to Jerusalem. This book takes place after the book of Daniel. (Approximately 525-586 B.C.)

The king of Persia releases the captives
Ezra 1:1-4

Note: While the Israelites were captives in Babylon, the Persians conquered them.

Thoughts and Notes:

_____

_____

_____

_____

_____

Day 111

Resistance to rebuilding the Temple
Ezra 4:4-5

Rebuilding the Temple is halted
Ezra 4:24

Thoughts and Notes:

_____

_____

_____

_____

_____

_____

_____

_____

_____

_____

_____

_____

_____

_____

_____

Day 112

The Temple is completed
Ezra 6:14

9 And let us not grow weary of doing good, for in due season we will reap, if we do not give up. 10 So then, as we have opportunity, let us do good to everyone, and especially to those who are of the household of faith.
Galatians 6:9-10

Ezra was a scribe
Ezra 7:6

Note: A scribe is a member of an educated class in ancient Israel through New Testament times studying the Scriptures and working as copyists, editors, teachers, and jurists.

Thoughts and Notes:

_____

_____

_____

_____

_____

_____

_____

_____

_____

_____

_____

Day 113

After they return, the people sin
Ezra 9:1-3

The people confess their sin
Ezra 10:1-4

8 If we say we have no sin, we deceive ourselves, and the truth is not in us. 9 If we confess our sins, he is faithful and just to forgive us our sins and to cleanse us from all unrighteousness. 10 If we say we have not sinned, we make him a liar, and his word is not in us.
I John 1:8-10

They take action to correct their sin
Ezra 10:19

Thoughts and Notes:

_____

_____

_____

_____

_____

_____

_____

_____

_____

Day 114

NEHEMIAH OVERVIEW

Title: Named after the man who is the main character of this book.

Author: Most likely Nehemiah, but there is no specific reference.

Audience: This is a historical book with no specific audience.

Historical setting: This book takes place after Ezra and chronicles Nehemiah returning to Jerusalem to rebuild the walls after the Babylonian conquest and 70-year captivity. (Nehemiah 8:9 "And Nehemiah, who was the governor, and Ezra the priest and scribe, and the Levites who taught the people said to all the people, "This day is holy to the Lord your God; do not mourn or weep." For all the people wept as they heard the words of the Law." (Approximately 445 - 423 B.C.)

Nehemiah fasts, prays, and confesses
Nehemiah 1:3-6

Thoughts and Notes:

_____

_____

_____

_____

_____

_____

Day 115

Nehemiah asks permission of King Artaxerxes to go and rebuild Jerusalem
Nehemiah 2:5

The start of rebuilding Jerusalem's walls
Nehemiah 3:1

The rebuilding of the wall is ridiculed
Nehemiah 4:1-2

Thoughts and Notes:

_____

_____

_____

_____

_____

_____

_____

_____

_____

_____

_____

_____

_____

_____

Day 116

Nehemiah's generosity
Nehemiah 5:14-19

17 "Let the one who boasts, boast in the Lord." 18 For it is not the one who commends himself who is approved, but the one whom the Lord commends.
II Corinthians 10:17-18

The wall is completed
Nehemiah 6:15-16

Thoughts and Notes:

_____

_____

_____

_____

_____

_____

_____

_____

_____

_____

_____

_____

_____

Day 117

Ezra reads the law
(*only read these 3 verses*)
Nehemiah 8:2-3, 6

1 I appeal to you therefore, brothers, by the mercies of God, to present your bodies as a living sacrifice, holy and acceptable to God, which is your spiritual worship.
Romans 12:1

The people confess their sins
Nehemiah 9:1-2

16 Therefore, confess your sins to one another and pray for one another, that you may be healed. The prayer of a righteous person has great power as it is working.
James 5:16

Thoughts and Notes:

_____

_____

_____

_____

_____

_____

_____

_____

_____

_____

_____

Day 118

Israelites separate from others
Nehemiah 13:1-3

33 Do not be deceived: "Bad company ruins good morals."
I Corinthians 15:33

Thoughts and Notes:

_____

_____

_____

_____

_____

_____

_____

_____

_____

_____

_____

_____

_____

_____

Day 119

ESTHER OVERVIEW

Title: Named after the woman who is the main character in this book.

Author: There is not a definite reference but possibly Mordecai, Esther's older cousin (Esther 9:20 "And Mordecai recorded these things and sent letters to all the Jews who were in all the provinces of King Ahasuerus, both near and far,").

Audience: This is a historical book with no specific audience.

Historical setting: During the reign of the Medes and Persians. Mordecai's great grandfather was taken away during the conquest of Jerusalem by Babylon. (Approximately 486-460 B.C.)

Thoughts and Notes:

_____

_____

_____

_____

_____

_____

_____

_____

_____

_____

Day 120

The Queen disobeys the King
Esther 1:12

The Queen's consequences for disobeying the king
Esther 1:19

Thoughts and Notes:

_____

_____

_____

_____

_____

_____

_____

_____

_____

_____

_____

_____

_____

_____

Day 121

The King looks for a new queen
Esther 2:4

31 "It was also said, 'Whoever divorces his wife, let him give her a certificate of divorce.' 32 But I say to you that everyone who divorces his wife, except on the ground of sexual immorality, makes her commit adultery, and whoever marries a divorced woman commits adultery.
Matthew 5:31-32

Esther is chosen to be the new queen
Esther 2:17

Thoughts and Notes:

_____

_____

_____

_____

_____

_____

_____

_____

_____

_____

_____

_____

Day 122

Esther had not yet revealed her heritage
Esther 2:20

Mordecai helps the King
Esther 2:21-23

Thoughts and Notes:

_____

_____

_____

_____

_____

_____

_____

_____

_____

_____

_____

_____

_____

_____

Day 123

Haman wants to kill all the Jews
Esther 3:12-13

Mordecai requests that Esther ask the King to save the Jews
Esther 4:12-14

1 Working together with Him, then, we appeal to you not to receive the grace of God in vain. 2 For He says,
"In a favorable time I listened to you, And in a day of salvation I have helped you."
Behold, now is the favorable time; behold, now is the day of salvation.
II Corinthians 6:1-2

Question for Thought: Ezra and the Israelites face opposition when rebuilding the temple. What kind of opposition do Christians today face? (Ezra 4:4-5)

Thoughts and Notes:

_____

_____

_____

_____

_____

_____

_____

_____

_____

Day 124

Esther's answer
Esther 4:16

Haman plots to kill Mordecai
Esther 5:14

Question for Thought: Esther risked her life to save her people; do you think you would have the courage to do the same? (Esther 4:16)

Thoughts and Notes:

_____

_____

_____

_____

_____

_____

_____

_____

_____

_____

_____

_____

Day 125

The King wants to honor Mordecai for his help
Esther 6:1-5

Haman thinks the honor is for him
Esther 6:6

Thoughts and Notes:

_____

_____

_____

_____

_____

_____

_____

_____

_____

_____

_____

_____

_____

_____

_____

Day 126

Haman suggests the form of honor
Esther 6:9

The Kings says the honor is for Mordecai
Esther 6:10

Thoughts and Notes:

_____

_____

_____

_____

_____

_____

_____

_____

_____

_____

_____

_____

_____

_____

Day 127

Esther tells the King of Haman's plot to kill the Jews
Esther 7:4-6

Haman's fate
Esther 7:10

19 Beloved, never avenge yourselves, but leave it to the wrath of God, for it is written, "Vengeance is mine, I will repay, says the Lord." 20 To the contrary, "if your enemy is hungry, feed him; if he is thirsty, give him something to drink; for by so doing you will heap burning coals on his head." 21 Do not be overcome by evil, but overcome evil with good.
Romans 12:19-21

Thoughts and Notes:

_____

_____

_____

_____

_____

_____

_____

_____

_____

_____

_____

Day 128

The Jews are saved
Esther 8:10-11

Mordecai's fate
Esther 10:2-3

10 Humble yourselves before the Lord, and he will exalt you.
James 4:10

Thoughts and Notes:

142

Day 129

JOB OVERVIEW

Title: Named after the man who is the primary figure in this book.

Reminder: Job is pronounced with a long O

Author: No reference is given.

Audience: This is a historical book with no specific audience.

Historical setting: Before the birth of Christ (Unknown B.C.)

Reminder: The next five books of the Old Testament are considered "Poetic Books" due to their writing styles.

Note: The book of Job is mainly an account of tragedies that befall Job, and the dialog with his three friends that follows; as well as God and Satan's involvement in the story.

Who was Job
Job 1:1-3

Thoughts and Notes:

_____

_____

_____

_____

_____

_____

Day 130

Satan and the Lord discuss Job
Job 1:9-12

Job loses his possessions and children
Job 1:13-19

Question for Thought: Why do you think God would allow Satan control over Job and his family? (Job 1:9-12)

Thoughts and Notes:

Day 131

Job's response to his losses
Job 1:20-21

The Lord and Satan discuss Job again
Job 2:3-6

Thoughts and Notes:

_____

_____

_____

_____

_____

_____

_____

_____

_____

_____

_____

_____

_____

_____

Day 132

Job's health is attacked
Job 2:7

Job's wife's gives him advice
Job 2:9

1 Blessed is the man
who walks not in the counsel of the wicked,
nor stands in the way of sinners,
nor sits in the seat of scoffers;
2 but his delight is in the law of the Lord,
and on his law he meditates day and night.
Psalm 1:1-2

Thoughts and Notes:

_____

_____

_____

_____

_____

_____

_____

_____

_____

_____

_____

Day 133

Job's response to his wife
Job 2:10

Job's three friends comfort him
Job 2:11-13

10 Do not forsake your friend and your father's friend,
and do not go to your brother's house in the day of your calamity.
Better is a neighbor who is near
than a brother who is far away.
Proverbs 27:10

Thoughts and Notes:

_____

_____

_____

_____

_____

_____

_____

_____

_____

_____

_____

_____

_____

Day 134

Job is depressed
Job 3:1-3

Eliphaz (a friend of Job's) thinks God is correcting Job
Job 5:17

Thoughts and Notes:

_____

_____

_____

_____

_____

_____

_____

_____

_____

_____

_____

_____

_____

_____

_____

Day 135

Job calls out to God
(*only read these 7 verses*)
Job 10:1-3, 10:7-9

Zopha (another friend of Job's) gives advice to Job
Job 11:13-15

Thoughts and Notes:

_____

_____

_____

_____

_____

_____

_____

_____

_____

_____

_____

_____

_____

_____

Day 136

Job is not comforted by his friends
Job 16:2

Bildad (Job's third friend) thinks Job Has sinned
Job 18:21

Thoughts and Notes:

_____

_____

_____

_____

_____

_____

_____

_____

_____

_____

_____

_____

_____

_____

_____

_____

Day 137

Job clings to hope in God
Job 23:10-12

4 But he answered, "It is written,

"'Man shall not live by bread alone,
    but by every word that comes from the mouth of God.'"
Matthew 4:4

The Lord questions Job
(*only read these 6 verses*)
Job 38:1-4, 40:2, 40:14

20 But who are you, O man, to answer back to God? Will what is molded say to its molder, "Why have you made me like this?" 21 Has the potter no right over the clay, to make out of the same lump one vessel for honorable use and another for dishonorable use? 22 What if God, desiring to show his wrath and to make known his power, has endured with much patience vessels of wrath prepared for destruction, 23 in order to make known the riches of his glory for vessels of mercy, which he has prepared beforehand for glory—
Romans 9:20-23

Thoughts and Notes:

_____

_____

_____

_____

_____

_____

_____

_____

151

Day 138

God mentions animals that are unknown today
(*only read these 2 verses*)
Job 40:15, 41:1

Job repents
Job 42:1-6

Thoughts and Notes:

_____

_____

_____

_____

_____

_____

_____

_____

_____

_____

_____

_____

_____

_____

_____

_____

Day 139

The Lord rebukes Job's friends
Job 42:7

The Lord restores Job's losses by doubling what he had before
Job 42:12-17

Thoughts and Notes:

_____

_____

_____

_____

_____

_____

_____

_____

_____

_____

_____

_____

_____

_____

Day 140

PSALMS OVERVIEW

Title: Psalms means "Praises" (in Hebrew). These are songs without notes.

Author: Most of the Psalms are written by King David (II Samuel 23:1)" Now these are the last words of David: The oracle of David, the son of Jesse, the oracle of the man who was raised on high, the anointed of the God of Jacob, the sweet psalmist of Israel:";

Some of the Psalms were written by the sons of Korah, "To the choirmaster. A Psalm of the Sons of Korah. (Psalm 47:1) Clap your hands, all peoples! Shout to God with loud songs of joy!;

Some of the Psalms were written by Asaph (II Chronicles 29-30) "And Hezekiah the king commanded the Levites to sing praises to the Lord with the words of David and Asaph the seer."

At least one Psalm was written by King David's son Solomon (Read Psalm 127)

Audience: The "body of believers" as seen in Psalm 136 where congregational participation is called for by the response "For His mercy endures forever" after each verse.

Historical Setting: Mainly the time of King David (since he wrote most of them). (Approximately 1000 B.C.)

Reminder: The cross references are considerably helpful in understanding the entire Bible. They link similar ideas, story lines, and prophetic writings, and show when and where prophesies are fulfilled.

Note: *There are no summaries listed with these scriptures, so you may move along more quickly and have better absorption. You may add your own heading.*

Thoughts and Notes:

_____

_____

_____

_____

_____

Day 141

Psalm 2:7-12

1 Long ago, at many times and in many ways, God spoke to our fathers by the prophets, 2 but in these last days he has spoken to us by his Son, whom he appointed the heir of all things, through whom also he created the world. 3 He is the radiance of the glory of God and the exact imprint of his nature, and he upholds the universe by the word of his power. After making purification for sins, he sat down at the right hand of the Majesty on high 4 having become as much superior to angels as the name he has inherited is more excellent than theirs. For to which of the angels did God ever say,

"You are My Son, Today I have begotten You"?
Or again,
"I will be to Him a Father, And He shall be to Me a Son"?

Hebrews 1:1-5

Thoughts and Notes:

_____

_____

_____

_____

_____

_____

_____

_____

_____

Day 142

15 But when the chief priests and the scribes saw the wonderful things that he did, and the children crying out in the temple, "Hosanna to the Son of David!" they were indignant, 16 and they said to him, "Do you hear what these are saying?" And Jesus said to them, "Yes; have you never read, "'Out of the mouth of infants and nursing babies you have prepared praise'?"
Matthew 21:15-16

Thoughts and Notes:

_____

_____

_____

_____

_____

_____

_____

_____

_____

_____

_____

_____

_____

Day 143

Psalm 16:8-10

25 For David says concerning him, "'I saw the Lord always before me, for he is at my right hand that I may not be shaken; 26 therefore my heart was glad, and my tongue rejoiced; my flesh also will dwell in hope. 27 For you will not abandon my soul to Hades, or let your Holy One see corruption. 28 You have made known to me the paths of life; you will make me full of gladness with your presence.'

29 "Brothers, I may say to you with confidence about the patriarch David that he both died and was buried, and his tomb is with us to this day. 30 Being therefore a prophet, and knowing that God had sworn with an oath to him that he would set one of his descendants on his throne, 31 he foresaw and spoke about the resurrection of the Christ, that he was not abandoned to Hades, nor did his flesh see corruption. 32 This Jesus God raised up, and of that we all are witnesses.

Acts 2:25-32

Thoughts and Notes:

_____

_____

_____

_____

_____

_____

_____

_____

_____

Day 144

24 And they crucified him and divided his garments among them, casting lots for them, to decide what each should take.

Mark 15:24

(*read the whole chapter*)
Psalm 23

14 I am the good shepherd. I know my own and my own know me, 15 just as the Father knows me and I know the Father; and I lay down my life for the sheep. 16 And I have other sheep that are not of this fold. I must bring them also, and they will listen to my voice. So there will be one flock, one shepherd.

John 10:14-16

Thoughts and Notes:

_____

_____

_____

_____

_____

_____

_____

_____

_____

_____

_____

Day 145

Psalm 33:8

3 And they sing the song of Moses, the servant of God, and the song of the Lamb, saying,
"Great and amazing are your deeds,
O Lord God the Almighty!
Just and true are your ways,
O King of the nations!
4 Who will not fear, O Lord,
and glorify your name?
For you alone are holy.
All nations will come
and worship you,
for your righteous acts have been revealed."
Revelation 15:3,4

Psalm 45:6-7

8 But of the Son He says,
"Your throne, O God, is forever and ever; the scepter of righteousness is the scepter of Your kingdom.
9 You have loved righteousness and hated wickedness; therefore God, your God, has anointed you with the oil of gladness beyond your companions."
Hebrews 1:8-9

Thoughts and Notes:

_____

_____

_____

_____

_____

Day 146

Psalm 69:20-21

34 they offered him wine to drink, mixed with gall, but when he tasted it, he would not drink it. 35 And when they had crucified him, they divided his garments among them by casting lots.
Matthew 27:34-35

Psalm 102:24-27

8 Jesus Christ is the same yesterday and today and forever.
Hebrews 13:8

Thoughts and Notes:

_____

_____

_____

_____

_____

_____

_____

_____

_____

_____

Day 147

Psalm 103:20

6 And again, when he brings the firstborn into the world, he says,

"Let all God's angels worship him."
7 Of the angels he says,

"He makes his angels winds,
and his ministers a flame of fire."

Hebrews 1:6-7

Thoughts and Notes:

Day 148

5 So also Christ did not exalt himself to be made a high priest, but was appointed by him who said to him,

> "You are my Son,
>   today I have begotten you";
> 6 as he says also in another place,

> "You are a priest forever,
>   after the order of Melchizedek."

7 In the days of his flesh, Jesus offered up prayers and supplications, with loud cries and tears, to him who was able to save him from death, and he was heard because of his reverence. 8 Although he was a son, he learned obedience through what he suffered. 9 And being made perfect, he became the source of eternal salvation to all who obey him, 10 being designated by God a high priest after the order of Melchizedek.

Hebrews 5:5-10

Thoughts and Notes:

_____

_____

_____

_____

_____

_____

_____

Day 149

Psalm 118:22-26

19 So then you are no longer strangers and aliens, but you are fellow citizens with the saints and members of the household of God, 20 built on the foundation of the apostles and prophets, Christ Jesus himself being the cornerstone, 21 in whom the whole structure, being joined together, grows into a holy temple in the Lord. 22 In him you also are being built together into a dwelling place for God by the Spirit.

Ephesians 2:19-22

Note: Saints are believers in Jesus.

Thoughts and Notes:

Day 150

Psalm 132:13-14

13 These all died in faith, not having received the things promised, but having seen them and greeted them from afar, and having acknowledged that they were strangers and exiles on the earth. 14 For people who speak thus make it clear that they are seeking a homeland. 15 If they had been thinking of that land from which they had gone out, they would have had opportunity to return. 16 But as it is, they desire a better country, that is, a heavenly one. Therefore God is not ashamed to be called their God, for he has prepared for them a city.
Hebrews 11:13-16

(Read the whole chapter)
Psalm 150

Thoughts and Notes:

_____

_____

_____

_____

_____

_____

_____

_____

_____

_____

Day 151

PROVERBS OVERVIEW

Title: Proverbs—The word Proverb is derived from two Latin words; "pro", meaning "for" and "verb", meaning "word", or taking the place of a many worded discourse.

Author: Proverbs Chapters 1-30 were written by King Solomon (Read Proverbs 1:1), Proverbs Chapter 30 was written by Agur (Read Proverbs 30:1), and Proverbs Chapter 31 was written by King Lemuel (Read Proverbs 31:1).

Audience: To anyone who reads them (Read Proverbs 1:2-4).

Historical setting: During King Solomon's (King David's son) time (Approximately 970 - 686 B.C.)

Note: *With the exception of the first entry there are no headings listed with these scriptures, and after the first five entries' there are no cross references, so you may move along more quickly and have better absorption. Feel free to add your own notes beside each entry.*

Why to trust the Lord
Proverbs 3:5-8

Thoughts and Notes:

_____

_____

_____

_____

_____

Day 152

Proverbs 4:7

7 In him we have redemption through his blood, the forgiveness of our trespasses, according to the riches of his grace, 8 which he lavished upon us, in all wisdom and insight 9 making known to us the mystery of his will, according to his purpose, which he set forth in Christ 10 as a plan for the fullness of time, to unite all things in him, things in heaven and things on earth.

Ephesians 1:7-10

Proverbs 5:3-6

21 I gave her time to repent, but she refuses to repent of her sexual immorality. 22 Behold, I will throw her onto a sickbed, and those who commit adultery with her I will throw into great tribulation, unless they repent of her works, 23 and I will strike her children dead. And all the churches will know that I am he who searches mind and heart, and I will give to each of you according to your works.

Revelation 2:21-23

Thoughts and Notes:

166

Day 153

Proverbs 6:6-11

8 But if anyone does not provide for his relatives, and especially for members of his household, he has denied the faith and is worse than an unbeliever.

I Timothy 5:8

Proverbs 10:18-21

26 If anyone thinks he is religious and does not bridle his tongue but deceives his heart, this person's religion is worthless.

James 1:26

Thoughts and Notes:

_____

_____

_____

_____

_____

_____

_____

_____

_____

_____

_____

Day 154

Proverbs 11:14

Proverbs 13:22

Thoughts and Notes:

_____

_____

_____

_____

_____

_____

_____

_____

_____

_____

_____

_____

_____

_____

Day 155

Proverbs 14:12

Proverbs 15:1

Thoughts and Notes:

_____

_____

_____

_____

_____

_____

_____

_____

_____

_____

_____

_____

_____

_____

_____

Day 156

Proverbs 15:16, 17

Proverbs 17:25

Thoughts and Notes:

_____

_____

_____

_____

_____

_____

_____

_____

_____

_____

_____

_____

_____

_____

_____

Day 157

Proverbs 18:22

Proverbs 19:11

Thoughts and Notes:

_____

_____

_____

_____

_____

_____

_____

_____

_____

_____

_____

_____

_____

Day 158

Proverbs 20:1

Proverbs 21:13

Thoughts and Notes:

_____

_____

_____

_____

_____

_____

_____

_____

_____

_____

_____

_____

_____

_____

Day 159

Proverbs 21:19

Proverbs 22:1

Thoughts and Notes:

_____

_____

_____

_____

_____

_____

_____

_____

_____

_____

_____

_____

_____

_____

Day 160

Proverbs 22:6

Proverbs 22:15

Thoughts and Notes:

_____

_____

_____

_____

_____

_____

_____

_____

_____

_____

_____

_____

_____

_____

©2013 Basic Bible Guide

Day 161

Proverbs 22:26, 27

Proverbs 23:29-33

Thoughts and Notes:

175

Day 162

Proverbs 25:8-10

Proverbs 27:1-2

Thoughts and Notes:

_____

_____

_____

_____

_____

_____

_____

_____

_____

_____

_____

_____

_____

_____

_____

Day 163

Proverbs 31:10

Proverbs 31:30

Thoughts and Notes:

_____

_____

_____

_____

_____

_____

_____

_____

_____

_____

_____

_____

_____

_____

Day 164

ECCLESIASTES OVERVIEW

Title: Ecclesiastes—means "the preacher" or one who speaks publicly in an assembly

Author: Probably King Solomon (Read Ecclesiastes 1:1)

Audience: No reference is given.

Historical setting: Not long after David was king in Jerusalem, during King Solomon's reign. (Approximately 930 B.C.)

An unfulfilled man
Ecclesiastes 1:2-4

58 Therefore, my beloved brothers, be steadfast, immovable, always abounding in the work of the Lord, knowing that in the Lord your labor is not in vain.
I Corinthians 15:58

Thoughts and Notes:

_____

_____

_____

_____

_____

_____

_____

_____

Day 165

He finds pleasure unsatisfying
Ecclesiastes 2:1

24 By faith Moses, when he was grown up, refused to be called the son of Pharaoh's daughter, 25 choosing rather to be mistreated with the people of God than to enjoy the fleeting pleasures of sin. 26 He considered the reproach of Christ greater wealth than the treasures of Egypt, for he was looking to the reward.
Hebrews 11:24-26

A time for everything
Ecclesiastes 3:1-8

Thoughts and Notes:

_____

_____

_____

_____

_____

_____

_____

_____

_____

_____

_____

Day 166

Wealth is unsatisfying
Ecclesiastes 5:10-11

19 "Do not lay up for yourselves treasures on earth, where moth and rust destroy and where thieves break in and steal, 20 but lay up for yourselves treasures in heaven, where neither moth nor rust destroys and where thieves do not break in and steal. 21 For where your treasure is, there your heart will be also.
Matthew 6:19-21

Many children and old age cannot satisfy
Ecclesiastes 6:3

Thoughts and Notes:

Day 167

Man has a free will
Ecclesiastes 7:29

Question for Thought: Do you think "men seeking out many schemes." means that man has a free will and we are all responsible for our own decisions? (Ecclesiastes 7:29)

Thoughts and Notes:

_____

_____

_____

_____

_____

_____

_____

_____

_____

_____

_____

_____

_____

Day 168

Ecclesiastes 8:16-17

33 Oh, the depth of the riches and wisdom and knowledge of God! How unsearchable are His judgments and how inscrutable are his ways!

34 "For who has known the mind of the Lord?
or who has become His counselor?"
35 "Or who has given a gift to him
that he might be repaid?"

36 For of Him and through Him and to Him are all things, to whom be glory forever. Amen.

Romans 11:33-36

Thoughts and Notes:

_____

_____

_____

_____

_____

_____

_____

_____

_____

_____

Day 169

Live good, even when you are young
Ecclesiastes 11:9-10

The conclusion
Ecclesiastes 12:13-14

12 And I saw the dead, great and small, standing before the throne, and books were opened. Then another book was opened, which is the book of life. And the dead were judged by what was written in the books, according to what they had done. 13 And the sea gave up the dead who were in it, Death and Hades gave up the dead who were in them, and they were judged, each one of them, according to what they had done. 14 Then Death and Hades were thrown into the lake of fire. This is the second death, the lake of fire. 15 And if anyone's name was not found written in the book of life, he was thrown into the lake of fire.
Revelation 20:12-15

Thoughts and Notes:

_____

_____

_____

_____

_____

_____

_____

_____

_____

Day 170

SONG OF SOLOMON OVERVIEW

Title: Named after verse 1 of this book (this book is also known as Song of Songs)

Author: Solomon (Read Song of Solomon 1:1)

Audience: No specific reference is given but as the title suggests this is a song (I Kings 4:30-32 "Thus Solomon's wisdom excelled the wisdom of all the men of the East and the all wisdom of Egypt. For he was wiser than all men- than Ethan the Ezrahite and Heman, Calcol, and Darda, the sons of Mahol; and his fame was in spread all surrounding nations. He spoke 3,000 proverbs and his songs were 1,005.")

Historical setting: During King Solomon's time. (Approximately 971-931 B.C.)

A woman loves a desirable man
Song of Solomon 1:2-3

Thoughts and Notes:

_____

_____

_____

_____

_____

_____

_____

_____

Day 171

The woman's beauty is poetically described
Song of Solomon 4:1-5

She searches for him
Song of Solomon 5:6-8

He says she is magnificent
Song of Solomon 6:8-10

Thoughts and Notes:

_____

_____

_____

_____

_____

_____

_____

_____

_____

_____

_____

_____

_____

_____

Day 172

She desires him strongly
Song of Solomon 7:10-13

They long for each other
Song of Solomon 8:10-14

7 Let us rejoice and exult and give Him the glory, for the marriage of the Lamb has come, and His Bride has made herself ready;8 it was granted her to clothe herself with fine linen, bright and pure" –

for the fine linen is the righteous deeds of the saints.

9 Then the angel said to me, "Write this: Blessed are those who are invited to the marriage supper of the Lamb." And he said to me, "These are the true words of God."
Revelation 19:7-9

Thoughts and Notes:

_____

_____

_____

_____

_____

_____

_____

_____

_____

186

Day 173

ISAIAH OVERVIEW

Title: Named after the prophet of this book

Note: Prophets are people who convey messages to others, as they have been revealed to them by God (usually concerning the future).

Author: Probably Isaiah (John 12:36-41 [36] While you have the light, believe in the light, that you may become sons of light." When Jesus had said these things, he departed and hid himself from them. [37] Though he had done so many signs before them, they still did not believe in him, [38] so that the word spoken by the prophet Isaiah might be fulfilled: "Lord, who has believed what he heard from us, and to whom has the arm of the Lord been revealed?" [39] Therefore they could not believe. For again Isaiah said, [40] "He has blinded their eyes and hardened their heart, lest they see with their eyes, and understand with their heart, and turn and I would heal them." [41] Isaiah said these things because he saw his glory and spoke of him.)

Audience: To Judah and Jerusalem and many other nations like Philistia (Read Isaiah 14:29), Tyre (Read Isaiah 23:1), and Babylon (Read Isaiah 47:1)

Historical setting: Approximately 100 years before Judah was taken by Babylon. (Approximately 740 - 680 B.C.)

Reminder: The next 17 books of the Old Testament are "Prophetic Books" which are written by prophets. These books are titled by the name of each of the profits that wrote them (such as Isaiah, Jonah, Joel and Obadiah). In these books you will find prophesies that are later fulfilled by Jesus in the New Testament, as can be seen in the cross references.

Thoughts and Notes:

_____

_____

_____

_____

_____

Day 174

A vision from God
Isaiah 1:1-2

The Lord's solution
Isaiah 1:24-26

God is displeased with certain behavior
Isaiah 5:20-23

Thoughts and Notes:

_____

_____

_____

_____

_____

_____

_____

_____

_____

_____

_____

_____

Day 175

A vision of the Lord
Isaiah 6:1-3

6 and before the throne there was as it were a sea of glass, like crystal.

And around the throne, on each side of the throne, are four living creatures, full of eyes in front and behind: 7 the first living creature like a lion, the second living creature like an ox, the third living creature with the face of a man, and the fourth living creature like an eagle in flight. 8 And the four living creatures, each of them with six wings, are full of eyes all around and within, and day and night they never cease to say,

"Holy, holy, holy, is the Lord God Almighty,
  who was and is and is to come!"
Revelation 4:6-8

Thoughts and Notes:

_____

_____

_____

_____

_____

_____

_____

_____

_____

Day 176

A sign from the Lord
Isaiah 7:14

20 But as he considered these things, behold, an angel of the Lord appeared to him in a dream, saying, "Joseph, son of David, do not fear to take Mary as your wife, for that which is conceived in her is from the Holy Spirit. 21 She will bear a son, and you shall call his name Jesus, for he will save his people from their sins." 22 All this took place to fulfill what the Lord had spoken by the prophet: 23 "Behold, the virgin shall conceive and bear a son, and they shall call his name Immanuel"(which means, God with us).
Matthew 1:20-23

Thoughts and Notes:

Day 177

A ruler is to come
Isaiah 9:6-7

A promise of coming peace
Isaiah 11:6-10

11 And again,

"Praise the Lord, all you Gentiles,
and let all the peoples extol him."
12 And again Isaiah says,

"The root of Jesse will come,
even he who arises to rule the Gentiles;
in him will the Gentiles hope."
Romans 15:11-12

Thoughts and Notes:

_____

_____

_____

_____

_____

_____

_____

_____

_____

Day 178

The fall of Lucifer
Isaiah 14:12-15

And He said to them, "I saw Satan fall like lightning from heaven.
Luke 10:18

God's people will be spared from His judgment of the Earth
Isaiah 26:20-21

Question for Thought: In the book of Isaiah we see God's judgment and salvation. How can God be two different extremes at the same time? (Isaiah 24:5-6 and Isaiah 49:6)

Thoughts and Notes:

_____

_____

_____

_____

_____

_____

_____

_____

_____

_____

_____

Day 179

The Lord God lays a foundation
Isaiah 28:16

9 And he began to tell the people this parable: "A man planted a vineyard and let it out to tenants and went into another country for a long while. 10 When the time came, he sent a servant to the tenants, so that they would give him some of the fruit of the vineyard. But the tenants beat him and sent him away empty-handed. 11 And he sent another servant. But they also beat and treated him shamefully, and sent him away empty-handed. 12 And he sent yet a third. This one also they wounded and cast out. 13 Then the owner of the vineyard said, 'What shall I do? I will send my beloved son; perhaps they will respect him.' 14 But when the tenants saw him, they said to themselves, 'This is the heir. Let us kill him, so that the inheritance may be ours.' 15 And they threw him out of the vineyard and killed him. What then will the owner of the vineyard do to them? 16 He will come and destroy those tenants and give the vineyard to others." When they heard this, they said, "Surely not!" 17 But he looked directly at them and said, "What then is this that is written:

"'The stone that the builders rejected
has become the cornerstone'?

18 Everyone who falls on that stone will be broken to pieces, and when it falls on anyone, it will crush him."
Luke 20:9-18

Thoughts and Notes:

_____

_____

_____

_____

_____

_____

Day 180

The Assyrians attack Judah
Isaiah 36:1

The king of Judah asks Isaiah to pray for Jerusalem
Isaiah 37:1-7

Thoughts and Notes:

_____

_____

_____

_____

_____

_____

_____

_____

_____

_____

_____

_____

_____

_____

Day 181

King Hezekiah, of Judah, also prays
Isaiah 37:20

The Lord answers their prayers
Isaiah 37:35-38

37 No, in all these things we are more than conquerors through him who loved us. 38 For I am sure that neither death nor life, nor angels nor rulers, nor things present nor things to come, nor powers, 39 nor height nor depth, nor anything else in all creation, will be able to separate us from the love of God in Christ Jesus our Lord.
Romans 8:37-39

Thoughts and Notes:

_____

_____

_____

_____

_____

_____

_____

_____

_____

_____

_____

Day 182

King Hezekiah shows all his treasures to Babylon
Isaiah 39:1-2

The result of the king's boasting
Isaiah 39:5-8

Thoughts and Notes:

_____

_____

_____

_____

_____

_____

_____

_____

_____

_____

_____

_____

_____

_____

_____

_____

_____

Day 183

There is only one God
Isaiah 44:6-8

Someone will bring God's salvation to the world
Isaiah 49:6

Thoughts and Notes:

_____

_____

_____

_____

_____

_____

_____

_____

_____

_____

_____

_____

_____

_____

_____

Day 184

The Lord's obedient servant
Isaiah 50:5-6

63 But Jesus remained silent. And the high priest said to him, "I adjure you by the living God, tell us if you are the Christ, the Son of God." 64 Jesus said to him, "You have said so. But I tell you, from now on you will see the Son of Man seated at the right hand of Power and coming on the clouds of heaven." 65 Then the high priest tore his robes and said, "He has uttered blasphemy. What further witnesses do we need? You have now heard his blasphemy. 66 What is your judgment?" They answered, "He deserves death." 67 Then they spit in his face and struck him. And some slapped him, 68 saying, "Prophesy to us, you Christ! Who is it that struck you?"

Matthew 26:63-68

The Lord's servant was wounded for us
Isaiah 53:5-6

24 He himself bore our sins in his body on the tree, that we might die to sin and live to righteousness. By his wounds you have been healed. 25 For you were straying like sheep, but have now returned to the Shepherd and Overseer of your souls.

I Peter 2:24-25

Thoughts and Notes:

_____

_____

_____

_____

_____

_____

_____

Day 185

The Lord's abundant mercy
Isaiah 55:6-9

This is the correct way to fast, and its results
Isaiah 58:6-10

Thoughts and Notes:

_____

_____

_____

_____

_____

_____

_____

_____

_____

_____

_____

_____

_____

_____

_____

Day 186

The Lord anointed someone to preach
Isaiah 61:1-2

14 And Jesus returned in the power of the Spirit to Galilee, and a report about him went out through all the surrounding country. 15 And he taught in their synagogues, being glorified by all.

16 And he came to Nazareth, where he had been brought up. And as was his custom, he went to the synagogue on the Sabbath day, and he stood up to read. 17 And the scroll of the prophet Isaiah was given to him. He unrolled the scroll and found the place where it was written,

18 "The Spirit of the Lord is upon me,
because he has anointed me
to proclaim good news to the poor.
He has sent me to proclaim liberty to the captives
and recovering of sight to the blind,
to set at liberty those who are oppressed,
19 to proclaim the year of the Lord's favor."

20 And he rolled up the scroll and gave it back to the attendant and sat down. And the eyes of all in the synagogue were fixed on him. 21 And he began to say to them, "Today this Scripture has been fulfilled in your hearing."
Luke 4:14-21

Rewards and punishment
Isaiah 66:14-15

Thoughts and Notes:

_____

_____

_____

_____

Day 187

JEREMIAH OVERVIEW

Title: Named after the prophet of this book

Author: Jeremiah (Read Jeremiah 1:1)

Audience: Israel (Jeremiah 2:4)

Historical setting: Jeremiah started prophesying about Judah's captivity in Babylon approximately before 30 years before it happened. (Approximately 627 - 580 B.C.)

The Lord's commission to Jeremiah
Jeremiah 1:4-8

7 for God gave us a spirit not of fear but of power and love and self-control.
II Timothy 1:7

Thoughts and Notes:

_____

_____

_____

_____

_____

_____

_____

Day 188

The Lord asks Israel to repent
Jeremiah 3:14

4 "What man of you, having a hundred sheep, if he has lost one of them, does not leave the ninety-nine in the open country, and go after the one that is lost, until he finds it? 5 And when he has found it, he lays it on his shoulders, rejoicing. 6 And when he comes home, he calls together his friends and his neighbors, saying to them, 'Rejoice with me, for I have found my sheep that was lost.' 7 Just so, I tell you, there will be more joy in heaven over one sinner who repents than over ninety-nine righteous persons who need no repentance.
Luke 15:4-7

Thoughts and Notes:

_____

_____

_____

_____

_____

_____

_____

_____

_____

Day 189

Israel refuses to repent
Jeremiah 5:3

The Lord does not accept Israel's sacrifices
Jeremiah 6:20

11 And when the Pharisees saw this, they said to his disciples, "Why does your teacher eat with tax collectors and sinners?" 12 But when he heard it, he said, "Those who are well have no need of a physician, but those who are sick. 13 Go and learn what this means, 'I desire mercy, and not sacrifice.' For I came not to call the righteous, but sinners."
Matthew 9:11-13

Thoughts and Notes:

Day 190

Jeremiah weeps for the people
Jeremiah 9:10

The people want to kill Jeremiah
Jeremiah 11:21

34 O Jerusalem, Jerusalem, the city that kills the prophets and stones those who are sent to it! How often would I have gathered your children together as a hen gathers her brood under her wings, and you were not willing!
Luke 13:34

Thoughts and Notes:

_____

_____

_____

_____

_____

_____

_____

_____

_____

_____

_____

_____

Day 191

The fate of Judah's children
Jeremiah 16:4

The Lord's sovereignty is illustrated
Jeremiah 18:3-6

Thoughts and Notes:

Day 192

The people's response
Jeremiah 18:12

The Lord will raise a king to judge the Earth
Jeremiah 23:5-6

11 Then I saw heaven opened, and behold, a white horse! The one sitting on it is called Faithful and True, and in righteousness he judges and makes war.
Revelation 19:11

Thoughts and Notes:

_____

_____

_____

_____

_____

_____

_____

_____

_____

_____

_____

_____

_____

Day 193

Jerusalem's prophets are unfaithful to the Lord
Jeremiah 23:14

Warning to false prophets
Jeremiah 23:25-29

18 I warn everyone who hears the words of the prophecy of this book: if anyone adds to them, God will add to him the plagues described in this book, 19 and if anyone takes away from the words of the book of this prophecy, God will take away his share in the tree of life and in the holy city, which are described in this book.
Revelation 22:18-19

Thoughts and Notes:

Day 194

Judah will be held captive in Babylon for 70 years
Jeremiah 25:11

The Lord instructs the captives to settle and multiply in Babylon
Jeremiah 29:4-6

Thoughts and Notes:

_____

_____

_____

_____

_____

_____

_____

_____

_____

_____

_____

_____

_____

Day 195

Jeremiah is commanded to make a journal, for the people will return
Jeremiah 30:2-3

The Lord will make a new covenant with Israel and Judah
Jeremiah 31:33-34

Thoughts and Notes:

Day 196

Jeremiah's words are read to all the people
Jeremiah 36:10

Jeremiah is imprisoned for speaking the Lord's word
Jeremiah 37:15

Thoughts and Notes:

_____

_____

_____

_____

_____

_____

_____

_____

_____

_____

_____

_____

_____

Day 197

King Zedekiah and Judah are conquered
Jeremiah 39:6-9

Jeremiah is released and goes free
Jeremiah 39:11-12

Babylon will be conquered
Jeremiah 50:1-2

Thoughts and Notes:

Day 198

The number of Jews taken into captivity
Jeremiah 52:28-30

The new king of Judah is treated well in Babylon
Jeremiah 52:33-34

Thoughts and Notes:

_____

_____

_____

_____

_____

_____

_____

_____

_____

_____

_____

_____

_____

_____

_____

Day 199

LAMENTATIONS OVERVIEW

Title: A lamentation is to "bewail", "alas", or "woe" a sad event or trying time.

Author: Probably Jeremiah (Read II Chronicles 35:25 "Jeremiah also lamented for Josiah. And to this day all the singing men and the singing women speak of Josiah in their lamentations.")

Audience: To the Lord (Read Lamentations 1:20)

Historical setting: After Jerusalem's fall to Babylon (Read Lamentations 1:7). (Approximately 587-516 B.C.)

Thoughts and Notes:

_____

_____

_____

_____

_____

_____

_____

_____

_____

_____

_____

_____

Day 200

The condition of Jerusalem
Lamentations 1:1-2

The Lord's judgment was executed
Lamentations 2:5

Thoughts and Notes:

_____

_____

_____

_____

_____

_____

_____

_____

_____

_____

_____

_____

_____

Day 201

In judgment the Lord is merciful
Lamentations 3:31-33

The Lord answers the prophet's plea
Lamentations 3:55-57

Thoughts and Notes:

_____

_____

_____

_____

_____

_____

_____

_____

_____

_____

_____

_____

_____

_____

Day 202

Further consequences of Jerusalem, and their cause
Lamentations 4:8-10

A sad prayer to the Lord
Lamentations 5:15-19

23 for all have sinned and fall short of the glory of God, 24 and are justified by his grace as a gift, through the redemption that is in Christ Jesus, 25 whom God put forward as a propitiation by his blood, to be received by faith. This was to show God's righteousness, because in his divine forbearance he had passed over former sins. 26 It was to show his righteousness at the present time, so that he might be just and the justifier of the one who has faith in Jesus.
Romans 3:23-26

Question for Thought: Jeremiah remembered Israel's affliction, and was distraught. However, he still had hope. What gave him this hope? (Lamentations 5:17-22)

Thoughts and Notes:

_____

_____

_____

_____

_____

_____

_____

_____

Day 203

EZEKIEL OVERVIEW

Title: Named after the prophet of this book

Author: Probably Ezekiel

Audience: The people of Israel

Historical setting: During Judah's captivity in Babylon after the prophet Jeremiah's book (Read Ezekiel 1:1-3). (Approximately 593-571 B.C.)

Thoughts and Notes:

_____

_____

_____

_____

_____

_____

_____

_____

_____

_____

_____

_____

Day 204

One of the visions Ezekiel the priest saw
Ezekiel 1:4-10

The Lord sends Ezekiel to speak to Israel
Ezekiel 2:3

1 Long ago, at many times and in many ways, God spoke to our fathers by the prophets, 2 but in these last days he has spoken to us by his Son, whom he appointed the heir of all things, through whom also he created the world.
Hebrews 1:1-2

Thoughts and Notes:

_____

_____

_____

_____

_____

_____

_____

_____

_____

_____

_____

_____

Day 205

A warning from the Lord
Ezekiel 3:17-21

19 My brothers, if anyone among you wanders from the truth and someone brings him back, 20 let him know that whoever brings back a sinner from his wandering will save his soul from death and will cover a multitude of sins.
James 5:19-20

Further warning for Israel
Ezekiel 6:1-3

Thoughts and Notes:

_____

_____

_____

_____

_____

_____

_____

_____

_____

_____

_____

_____

_____

Day 206

Ezekiel sees Israel sin
Ezekiel 8:9-12

God will restore Israel and they will repent
Ezekiel 11:17-18

Thoughts and Notes:

_____

_____

_____

_____

_____

_____

_____

_____

_____

_____

_____

_____

_____

_____

Day 207

A warning to false prophets
Ezekiel 13:2-3

21 And then if anyone says to you, 'Look, here is the Christ!' or 'Look, there he is!' do not believe it. 22 For false christs and false prophets will arise and perform signs and wonders, to lead astray, if possible, the elect.
Mark 13:21-22

God is jealous for his people
Ezekiel 16:36-38

2 For I feel a divine jealousy for you, since I betrothed you to one husband, to present you as a pure virgin to Christ. 3 But I am afraid that as the serpent deceived Eve by his cunning, your thoughts will be led astray from a sincere and pure devotion to Christ.
II Corinthians 11:2-3

Thoughts and Notes:

_____

_____

_____

_____

_____

_____

_____

_____

_____

Day 208

God is jealous for his people
Ezekiel 16:36-38

2 For I feel a divine jealousy for you, since I betrothed you to one husband, to present you as a pure virgin to Christ. 3 But I am afraid that as the serpent deceived Eve by his cunning, your thoughts will be led astray from a sincere and pure devotion to Christ.
II Corinthians 11:2-3

Each person is responsible for his own actions
Ezekiel 18:20

Thoughts and Notes:

_____

_____

_____

_____

_____

_____

_____

_____

_____

_____

_____

_____

Day 209

Ezekiel is a sign to Israel
Ezekiel 24:24

18 So the Jews said to him, "What sign do you show us for doing these things?" 19 Jesus answered them, "Destroy this temple, and in three days I will raise it up." 20 The Jews then said, "It has taken forty-six years to build this temple, and will you raise it up in three days?" 21 But he was speaking about the temple of his body. 22 When therefore he was raised from the dead, his disciples remembered that he had said this, and they believed the Scripture and the word that Jesus had spoken.
John 2:18-22

The greatness of a king and his sin
Ezekiel 28:12-15

Trusting in man's righteousness
Ezekiel 33:12-13

2 For I bear them witness that they have a zeal for God, but not according to knowledge. 3 For, being ignorant of the righteousness of God, and seeking to establish their own, they did not submit to God's righteousness. 4 For Christ is the end of the law for righteousness to everyone who believes.
Romans 10:2-4

Thoughts and Notes:

_____

_____

_____

_____

_____

Day 210

God will shepherd his people
Ezekiel 34:11-12

24 So the Jews gathered around him and said to him, "How long will you keep us in suspense? If you are the Christ, tell us plainly." 25 Jesus answered them, "I told you, and you do not believe. The works that I do in my Father's name bear witness about me, 26 but you do not believe because you are not among my sheep. 27 My sheep hear my voice, and I know them, and they follow me. 28 I give them eternal life, and they will never perish, and no one will snatch them out of my hand.
John 10:24-28

Gog will attack Israel in the future
Ezekiel 38:14-16

7 And when the thousand years are ended, Satan will be released from his prison 8 and will come out to deceive the nations that are at the four corners of the earth, Gog and Magog, to gather them for battle; their number is like the sand of the sea. 9 And they marched up over the broad plain of the earth and surrounded the camp of the saints and the beloved city, but fire came down from heaven and consumed them,
Revelation 20:7-9

Thoughts and Notes:

_____

_____

_____

_____

_____

_____

Day 211

DANIEL OVERVIEW

Title: Named after the prophet of this book

Author: Daniel (Read Daniel 7:15 ""As for me, Daniel, my spirit within me was anxious, and the visions of my head alarmed me.")

Audience: Not mentioned in this book

Historical setting: During Judah's captivity in Babylon, who were also known as the Chaldeans. This book takes place after the book of Jeremiah (Read Daniel 9:1-2 "In the first year of Darius the son of Ahasuerus, by descent a Mede, who was made king over the realm of the Chaldeans— 2 in the first year of his reign, I, Daniel, perceived in the books the number of years that, according to the word of the Lord to Jeremiah the prophet, must pass before the end of the desolations of Jerusalem, namely, seventy years."). (Approximately 605-536 B.C.)

King Nebuchadnezzar chooses Daniel to serve him
Daniel 1:17-19

Daniel interprets the king's dream, and gives the credit to God
Daniel 2:44-45

Thoughts and Notes:

_____

_____

_____

_____

_____

_____

Day 212

Three captives disobey the King
Daniel 3:14-23

God delivers them
Daniel 3:25-26

Question for Thought: Daniel disobeys the king, yet remains obedient to God. Do you think it is okay to break laws made here on Earth by authorities if it goes against God's law? (Daniel 3:14-18)

Thoughts and Notes:

_____

_____

_____

_____

_____

_____

_____

_____

_____

_____

_____

_____

Day 213

The pride of King Nebuchadnezzar
Daniel 4:30-33

King Nebuchadnezzar is restored
Daniel 4:34-37

6 But he gives more grace. Therefore it says, "God opposes the proud, but gives grace to the humble." 7 Submit yourselves therefore to God. Resist the devil, and he will flee from you. 8 Draw near to God, and he will draw near to you. Cleanse your hands, you sinners, and purify your hearts, you double-minded. 9 Be wretched and mourn and weep. Let your laughter be turned to mourning and your joy to gloom. 10 Humble yourselves before the Lord, and he will exalt you.
James 4:6-10

Thoughts and Notes:

Day 214

Daniel delivered from the lions
Daniel 6:22-24

Daniel humbles himself for the people of Israel
Daniel 9:2-6

Thoughts and Notes:

_____

_____

_____

_____

_____

_____

_____

_____

_____

_____

_____

_____

_____

_____

_____

_____

Day 215

A vision of Daniel's is explained by Gabriel
Daniel 9:24-27

Another vision explained
Daniel 12:7

10 And I heard a loud voice in heaven, saying, "Now the salvation and the power and the kingdom of our God and the authority of his Christ have come, for the accuser of our brothers has been thrown down, who accuses them day and night before our God. 11 And they have conquered him by the blood of the Lamb and by the word of their testimony, for they loved not their lives even unto death. 12 Therefore, rejoice, O heavens and you who dwell in them! But woe to you, O earth and sea, for the devil has come down to you in great wrath, because he knows that his time is short!"

13 And when the dragon saw that he had been thrown down to the earth, he pursued the woman who had given birth to the male child. 14 But the woman was given the two wings of the great eagle so that she
might fly from the serpent into the wilderness, to the place where she is to be nourished for a time, and times, and half a time.
Revelation 12:10-14

Thoughts and Notes:

_____

_____

_____

_____

_____

_____

Day 216

HOSEA OVERVIEW

Title: Named after the prophet of this book

Author: Probably Hosea (Read Hosea 1:1)

Audience: Israel

Historical setting: Hosea was a prophet to Israel, not Judah, and this book takes place during the time of Israel's destruction (Read Hosea 1:6). (Approximately 753-687 B.C.)

Reminder: Several of the prophetic books overlap in time, or are not in chronological order. Judah was conquered after Hosea by the Babylonians.

The Lord tells Hosea to take a harlot for a wife
Hosea 1:2-4

Thoughts and Notes:

_____

_____

_____

_____

_____

_____

_____

_____

Day 217

A future relationship with the Lord
Hosea 2:18-20

Israel rejects God
Hosea 8:2-4

Thoughts and Notes:

_____

_____

_____

_____

_____

_____

_____

_____

_____

_____

_____

_____

_____

_____

_____

_____

Day 218

The Lord's love for Israel
Hosea 11:1-4

Be wise and walk in the ways of the Lord
Hosea 14:9

4 Abide in me, and I in you. As the branch cannot bear fruit by itself, unless it abides in the vine, neither can you, unless you abide in me. 5 I am the vine; you are the branches. Whoever abides in me and I in him, he it is that bears much fruit, for apart from me you can do nothing.
John 15:4-5

Thoughts and Notes:

_____

_____

_____

_____

_____

_____

_____

_____

_____

_____

_____

Day 219

JOEL OVERVIEW

Title: Named after the prophet of this book

Author: Thought to be Joel (Read Joel 1:1)

Audience: The people of Zion (Read Joel 2:32 "And it shall come to pass that everyone who calls on the name of the Lord shall be saved. For in Mount Zion and in Jerusalem there shall be those who escape, as the Lord has said, and among the survivors shall be those whom the Lord calls.")

Historical setting: It's not certain from the text. (Approximately 1050-590 B.C.)

Note: Zion is synonymous with Jerusalem, the capital of the Israelites.

Thoughts and Notes:

_____

_____

_____

_____

_____

_____

_____

_____

_____

Day 220

The land is laid to waste
Joel 1:3-4

A horrible day is coming
Joel 2:1-2

Thoughts and Notes:

_____

_____

_____

_____

_____

_____

_____

_____

_____

_____

_____

_____

_____

_____

Day 221

God will pour out His Spirit on people
Joel 2:28-29

14 But Peter, standing with the eleven, lifted up his voice and addressed them: "Men of Judea and all who dwell in Jerusalem, let this be known to you, and give ear to my words. 15 For these people are not drunk, as you suppose, since it is only the third hour of the day. 16 But this is what was uttered through the prophet Joel:

17 "'And in the last days it shall be, God declares, that I will pour out my Spirit on all flesh, and your sons and your daughters shall prophesy, and your young men shall see visions, and your old men shall dream dreams; 18 even on my male servants and female servants in those days I will pour out my Spirit, and they shall prophesy. 19 And I will show wonders in the heavens above and signs on the earth below, blood, and fire, and vapor of smoke; 20 the sun shall be turned to darkness and the moon to blood, before the day of the Lord comes, the great and magnificent day. 21 And it shall come to pass that everyone who calls upon the name of the Lord shall be saved.'
Acts 2:14-21

The Lord will shield His people in Zion
Joel 3:16-17

Thoughts and Notes:

_____

_____

_____

_____

_____

Day 222

AMOS OVERVIEW

Title: Named after the prophet of this book

Author: Thought to be Amos (Read Amos 1:1)

Audience: The people of Israel

Historical setting: During King Uzziah of Judah's reign, while Jeroboam was king of Israel; which was during the same time as the prophet Hosea. (Approximately 793-739 B.C.)

Thoughts and Notes:

_____

_____

_____

_____

_____

_____

_____

_____

_____

_____

_____

_____

Day 223

God punishes his children
Amos 3:1-2

---

5 And have you forgotten the exhortation that addresses you as sons? "My son, do not regard lightly the discipline of the Lord, nor be weary when reproved by him. 6 For the Lord disciplines the one he loves, and chastises every son whom he receives." 7 It is for discipline that you have to endure. God is treating you as sons. For what son is there whom his father does not discipline? 8 If you are left without discipline, in which all have participated, then you are illegitimate children and not sons.9 Besides this, we have had earthly fathers who disciplined us and we respected them. Shall we not much more be subject to the Father of spirits and live?
Hebrews 12:5-9

The Lord can change future events because of prayer
Amos 7:4-6

Question for Thought: God's current actions are changed due to a man's prayer. Do you believe prayer can really change agendas? (Amos 7:4-6)

Thoughts and Notes:

_____

_____

_____

_____

_____

_____

Day 224

The word of the Lord will cease for a time
Amos 8:11-12

Israel will be restored to its land forever
Amos 9:14-15

Thoughts and Notes:

_____

_____

_____

_____

_____

_____

_____

_____

_____

_____

_____

_____

_____

_____

Day 225

OBADIAH OVERVIEW

Title: Named after the prophet of this book

Author: Thought to be Obadiah (Read Obadiah 1:1)

Audience: Edom, also known as Esau

Note: Esau, whose name was changed to Edom, was Jacob's twin brother, Abraham's grandchildren.

Historical setting: After the fall of Judah to Babylon. (Approximately 586 B.C.)

Edom's pride brings them down
Obadiah 1:3

Edom (or Esau) chastised for gloating over his brother Jacob's (or Israel's) calamity
Obadiah 1:10-12

Thoughts and Notes:

_____

_____

_____

_____

_____

_____

Day 226

JONAH OVERVIEW

Title: Named after the prophet of this book

Author: Thought to be Jonah (Read Jonah 1:1)

Audience: Not stated

Historical setting: During king of Judah, Amaziah's reign and King of
Israel Jeroboam's reign, who Jonah prophesied "according to
the word of the Lord" (As seen in II Kings 14:23-25, read these
versus later). (Approximately 782-753 B.C.)

God's instruction and Jonah's disobedience
Jonah 1:2-3

Question for Thought: If Jonah believed in God, why did he think he
could hide from God? (Jonah 1:2-3)

Thoughts and Notes:

_____

_____

_____

_____

_____

_____

_____

_____

Day 227

Jonah's consequence for his disobedience
Jonah 1:15-17

Jonah prays and is saved
Jonah 2:7-10

Thoughts and Notes:

_____

_____

_____

_____

_____

_____

_____

_____

_____

_____

_____

_____

_____

_____

Day 228

Nineveh repents and God spared them
Jonah 3:6-10

10 For godly grief produces a repentance that leads to salvation without regret,
whereas worldly grief produces death.
II Corinthians 7:10

The reason Jonah fled to Tarshish, disobeying the Lord
Jonah 4:1-2

Thoughts and Notes:

Day 229

The Lord is merciful
Jonah 4:6-11

38 Then some of the scribes and Pharisees answered him, saying, "Teacher, we wish to see a sign from you." 39 But he answered them, "An evil and adulterous generation seeks for a sign, but no sign will be given to it except the sign of the prophet Jonah. 40 For just as Jonah was three days and three nights in the belly of the great fish, so will the Son of Man be three days and three nights in the heart of the earth. 41 The men of Nineveh will rise up at the judgment with this generation and condemn it, for they repented at the preaching of Jonah, and behold, something greater than Jonah is here.
Matthew 12:38-41

Thoughts and Notes:

_____

_____

_____

_____

_____

_____

_____

_____

_____

_____

Day 230

MICAH OVERVIEW

Title: Named after the prophet of this book

Author: Thought to be Micah (Read Micah 1:1)

Audience: All the earth (Read Micah 1:2)

Historical setting: Micah prophesied approximately 120 years before Judah's captivity in Babylon, during the time of the prophet Isaiah. (Approximately 715-687 B.C.)

Thoughts and Notes:

_____

_____

_____

_____

_____

_____

_____

_____

_____

_____

_____

_____

Day 231

Woe to evildoers
Micah 2:1

An ancient ruler will come from Bethlehem
Micah 5:2

4 And Joseph also went up from Galilee, from the town of Nazareth, to Judea, to the city of David, which is called Bethlehem, because he was of the house and lineage of David, 5 to be registered with Mary, his betrothed, who was with child. 6 And while they were there, the time came for her to give birth. 7 And she gave birth to her firstborn son and wrapped him in swaddling cloths and laid him in a manger, because there was no place for them in the inn.
Luke 2:4-7

Thoughts and Notes:

_____

_____

_____

_____

_____

_____

_____

_____

_____

_____

Day 232

The Lord's requirements
Micah 6:7-8

The Lord is compassionate
Micah 7:18-19

Blessed be the God and Father of our Lord Jesus Christ, the Father of mercies and God of all comfort, who comforts us in all our tribulation, that we may be able to comfort those who are in any trouble, with the comfort with which we ourselves are comforted by God.
II Corinthians 1:3-4

Thoughts and Notes:

_____

_____

_____

_____

_____

_____

_____

_____

_____

_____

_____

_____

Day 233

NAHUM OVERVIEW

Title: Named after the prophet of this book

Author: Thought to be Nahum (Read Nahum 1:1)

Audience: Nineveh
(Read Nahum 3:7 "And all who look at you will shrink from you and say,
"Wasted is Nineveh; who will grieve for her?"
Where shall I seek comforters for you?")

Historical setting: After Nineveh repented from Jonah's preaching but went back to their sins and ended up being destroyed in the end (Approximately 750-664 B.C.)

God's vengeance
Nahum 1:2-3

Thoughts and Notes:

_____

_____

_____

_____

_____

_____

_____

Day 234

Nineveh is a desolate waste
Nahum 2:8-10

Nineveh's sins
Nahum 3:1-4

Thoughts and Notes:

_____

_____

_____

_____

_____

_____

_____

_____

_____

_____

_____

_____

_____

_____

Day 235

HABAKKUK OVERVIEW

Title: Named after the prophet of this book

Author: Thought to be Habakkuk (Read Habakkuk 1:1)

Audience: The Lord

Historical setting: Before the Babylonian invasion of Judah
        (Approximately 640-609 B.C.)

Thoughts and Notes:

_____

_____

_____

_____

_____

_____

_____

_____

_____

_____

_____

Day 236

The prophets plea and the Lord's reply
Habakkuk 1:2-5

The just shall live by faith
Habakkuk 2:2-4

11 Now it is evident that no one is justified before God by the law, for "The righteous shall live by faith." 12 But the law is not of faith, rather "The one who does them shall live by them." 13 Christ redeemed us from the curse of the law by becoming a curse for us—for it is written, "Cursed is everyone who is hanged on a tree"— 14 so that in Christ Jesus the blessing of Abraham might come to the Gentiles, so that we might receive the promised Spirit through faith.
Galatians 3:11-14

Thoughts and Notes:

Day 237

Habakkuk prays
Habakkuk 3:2

A song of faith to the Lord
Habakkuk 3:17-19

11 Not that I am speaking of being in need, for I have learned in whatever situation I am to be content. 12 I know how to be brought low, and I know how to abound. In any and every circumstance, I have learned the secret of facing plenty and hunger, abundance and need. 13 I can do all things through him who strengthens me.

Philippians 4:11-13

Thoughts and Notes:

_____

_____

_____

_____

_____

_____

_____

_____

_____

_____

_____

_____

Day 238

ZEPHANIAH OVERVIEW

Title: Named after the prophet of this book

Author: Thought to be Zephaniah (Read Zephaniah 1:1)

Audience: Judah (Read Zephaniah 1:4)

Historical setting: During the days of Josiah, King of Judah and the prophet Jeremiah. (Approximately 640-609 B.C.)

Seek the Lord to escape judgment
Zephaniah 2:3

The Lord will deliver His people
Zephaniah 3:17-20

Thoughts and Notes:

_____

_____

_____

_____

_____

_____

_____

Day 239

HAGGAI OVERVIEW

Title: Named after the prophet of this book

Author: Thought to be Haggai (Read Haggai 1:1)

Audience: Zerubbabel, the governor of Judah and Joshua, the high priest

Historical setting: After the captivity of Judah in Babylon, and their release from captivity, during the same time as the book or person, Ezra. (Approximately 520 B.C.)

Thoughts and Notes:

_____

_____

_____

_____

_____

_____

_____

_____

_____

_____

_____

Day 240

The people build their houses but not the temple
Haggai 1:2-4

The people obeyed and started building the temple
Haggai 1:12-14

Thoughts and Notes:

_____

_____

_____

_____

_____

_____

_____

_____

_____

_____

_____

_____

_____

Day 241

ZECHARIAH OVERVIEW

Title: Named after the prophet of this book

Author: Thought to be Zechariah (Read Zechariah 1:1)

Audience: Jerusalem

Historical setting: Zechariah was in Jerusalem with Haggai and Ezra after the captivity of Judah in Babylon. (Approximately 538-517 B.C.)

Satan is rebuked
Zechariah 3:1-2

9 But when the archangel Michael, contending with the devil, was disputing about the body of Moses, he did not presume to pronounce a blasphemous judgment, but said, "The Lord rebuke you."
Jude 1:9

Thoughts and Notes:

_____

_____

_____

_____

_____

_____

_____

Day 242

One of Zechariah's visions
Zechariah 4:2-6

Fast (to abstain from food while praying and seeking God's favor) with a true heart
Zechariah 7:5-10

16 "And when you fast, do not look gloomy like the hypocrites, for they disfigure their faces that their fasting may be seen by others. Truly, I say to you, they have received their reward. 17 But when you fast, anoint your head and wash your face, 18 that your fasting may not be seen by others but by your Father who is in secret. And your Father who sees in secret will reward you.
Matthew 6:16-18

Thoughts and Notes:

_____

_____

_____

_____

_____

_____

_____

_____

_____

_____

Day 243

As a prophesy, a price set on the Lord
Zechariah 11:12-13

3 Then when Judas, his betrayer, saw that Jesus was condemned, he changed his mind and brought back the thirty pieces of silver to the chief priests and the elders, 4 saying, "I have sinned by betraying innocent blood." They said, "What is that to us? See to it yourself."
Matthew 27:3-4

The Lord will come with His saints
Zechariah 14:5

Thoughts and Notes:

_____

_____

_____

_____

_____

_____

_____

_____

_____

_____

_____

Day 244

MALACHI OVERVIEW

Title: Named after the prophet of this book

Author: Thought to be Malachi (Read Malachi 1:1)

Audience: Israel

Historical setting: After the exiles of the Babylonian captivity returned to Judah. This was also after Edom, or Esau, was overthrown (Read Malachi 1:4). (Approximately 520-511 B.C.)

A messenger sent before the Lord
Malachi 3:1

Thoughts and Notes:

_____

_____

_____

_____

_____

_____

_____

_____

_____

_____

Day 245

Robbing God of tithes (one tenth of your produce or earnings that go to the Lord, read Leviticus 27:30-33 another time)
Malachi 3:8-10

23 "Woe to you, scribes and Pharisees, hypocrites! For you tithe mint and dill and cumin, and have neglected the weightier matters of the law: justice and mercy and faithfulness. These you ought to have done, without neglecting the others.
Matthew 23:23

A burning day is coming
Malachi 4:1-2

Question for Thought: God states that his people are "robbing" him by not bringing their "tithes" (a 10th of their wages) to the "storehouse". Why would God want people to give? (Malachi 3:8-10)

Thoughts and Notes:

_____

_____

_____

_____

_____

_____

_____

_____

_____

_____

Day 246

Reminder: <u>The New Testament</u> is the second section of the Bible and was originally written in the Greek language. It is comprised of 27 books that cover the life, ministry and purpose of Jesus, as well as the ministry of Jesus' first believers (also known as followers, disciples or Christians, which means "little Christ" or Christ-like). It includes letters of instruction and exhortation to the growing groups of believers around the world. The New Testament concludes with events and instructions for the end of this world and the beginning of a new world.

MATTHEW OVERVIEW

Title: Named after one of Jesus' 12 Disciples

Note: A disciple is one of Jesus' chosen 12 inner circle of followers/believers who accepted and helped spread Jesus' teachings.

Author: Thought to be Matthew

Audience: The text does not say

Historical setting: During Jesus' life, after Jesus was killed, and rose to life again.
(Approximately 0-33 A.D.)

Reminder: The first four books of the New Testament are known as the "Gospels", which means "good news". They cover the life of Jesus on Earth. They are written (and titled) by four different people (Matthew, Mark, Luke and John).

Note: Even though all four Gospels cover Jesus' life they have different perspectives, and include different details.

Thoughts and Notes:

_____

_____

_____

_____

_____

Day 247

Genealogy, or lineage, of Jesus
(*only read these two verses*)
Matthew 1:1 and 17

Jesus is born
Matthew 1:18-23

Reminder: The cross references are considerably helpful in understanding the entire Bible. They link similar ideas, story lines, and prophetic writings, and show when and where prophesies are fulfilled.

Thoughts and Notes:

_____

_____

_____

_____

_____

_____

_____

_____

_____

_____

_____

_____

Day 248

The devil tries to tempt Jesus
Matthew 4:1-11

3 And he humbled you and let you hunger and fed you with manna, which you did not know, nor did your fathers know, that he might make you know that man does not live by bread alone, but man lives by every word that comes from the mouth of the Lord.
Deuteronomy 8:3

Jesus fulfills the law and prophesy
Matthew 5:17-18

Thoughts and Notes:

_____

_____

_____

_____

_____

_____

_____

_____

_____

_____

_____

Day 249

Jesus teaches on prayer
Matthew 6:5-15

A miracle for Peter's mother-in-law
Matthew 8:14-15

Note: Peter was one of Jesus' 12 disciples

Thoughts and Notes:

_____

_____

_____

_____

_____

_____

_____

_____

_____

_____

_____

_____

_____

_____

_____

Day 250

Acknowledge or deny Jesus
Matthew 10:32-33

Finding or losing your life
Matthew 10:38-39

Thoughts and Notes:

_____

_____

_____

_____

_____

_____

_____

_____

_____

_____

_____

_____

_____

_____

Day 251

Do not speak against the Holy Spirit
Matthew 12:30-32

Reminder: The Holy Spirit is the spirit of God which is his promise that he gives to believers of Jesus as proof of His forgiveness and their salvation.
(Read Acts 2:32-33 "32 This Jesus God raised up, and of that we all are witnesses. 33 Being therefore exalted at the right hand of God, and having received from the Father the promise of the Holy Spirit, he has poured out this that you yourselves are seeing and hearing."
And Read Ephesians 4:30 "And do not grieve the Holy Spirit of God, with whom you were sealed for the day of redemption.")

Thoughts and Notes:

_____

_____

_____

_____

_____

_____

_____

_____

_____

_____

_____

_____

_____

Day 252

21 So the Lord God caused a deep sleep to fall upon the man, and while he slept took one of his ribs and closed up its place with flesh. 22 And the rib that the Lord God had taken from the man he made into a woman and brought her to the man. 23 Then the man said,

"This at last is bone of my bones
and flesh of my flesh;
she shall be called Woman,
because she was taken out of Man."

24 Therefore a man shall leave his father and his mother and hold fast to his wife, and they shall become one flesh.

Genesis 2:21-24

Thoughts and Notes:

_____

_____

_____

_____

_____

_____

_____

_____

_____

_____

Day 253

How to be great
Matthew 20:25-28

The first or greatest commandment
Matthew 22:36-40

5 You shall love the Lord your God with all your heart and with all your soul and with all your might. 6 And these words that I command you today shall be on your heart. 7 You shall teach them diligently to your children, and shall talk of them when you sit in your house, and when you walk by the way, and when you lie down, and when you rise.
Deuteronomy 6:5-7

Thoughts and Notes:

_____

_____

_____

_____

_____

_____

_____

_____

_____

_____

_____

Day 254

Question for Thought: Jesus rebukes the religious leaders of his day, calling them hypocrites. Do you think Jesus would have the same attitude towards some religious leaders today? (Matthew 23:13-15)

Thoughts and Notes:

_____

_____

_____

_____

_____

_____

_____

_____

_____

_____

_____

_____

_____

Day 255

Warnings of great tribulation
Matthew 24:21-27

Who goes to Heaven or Hell
Matthew 25:31-46

7 But the Lord sits enthroned forever;
he has established his throne for justice,
8 and he judges the world with righteousness;
he judges the peoples with uprightness.
Psalm 9:7-8

Thoughts and Notes:

_____

_____

_____

_____

_____

_____

_____

_____

_____

_____

_____

_____

Day 256

Jesus dies on the cross
Matthew 27:50-51

Note: Crucifixion was a Roman technique of slowly and painfully executing the condemned by tying or nailing them to a large wooden cross and leaving them to die.

33 And you shall hang the veil from the clasps, and bring the ark of the testimony in there within the veil. And the veil shall separate for you the Holy Place from the Most Holy.

Exodus 26:33

Jesus rises from the dead
Matthew 28:2-7

Thoughts and Notes:

_____

_____

_____

_____

_____

_____

_____

_____

_____

_____

_____

_____

Day 257

Jesus' instructions or commission to His followers
Matthew 28:16-20

13 "I saw in the night visions,

and behold, with the clouds of heaven
   there came one like a son of man,
and he came to the Ancient of Days
   and was presented before him.
14 And to him was given dominion
   and glory and a kingdom,
that all peoples, nations, and languages
   should serve him;
his dominion is an everlasting dominion,
   which shall not pass away,
and his kingdom one
   that shall not be destroyed.
Daniel 7:13-14

Thoughts and Notes:

_____

_____

_____

_____

_____

_____

_____

_____

Day 258

MARK OVERVIEW

Title: Named after a believer of Jesus (Read Acts 12:12 "When he realized this, he went to the house of Mary, the mother of John whose other name was Mark, where many were gathered together and were praying.")

Author: Thought to be Mark

Audience: The text does not say

Historical setting: During Jesus' life, death and resurrection (Mark 16:6 "And he said to them, "Do not be alarmed. You seek Jesus of Nazareth, who was crucified. He has risen; he is not here. See the place where they laid him."). (Approximately 0-33 A.D.)

Jesus is baptized
Mark 1:9-11

Thoughts and Notes:

_____

_____

_____

_____

_____

_____

_____

_____

Day 259

A paralytic is forgiven and healed by Jesus
Mark 2:3-12

Lord of the Sabbath (the seventh day of the week on which God rested and made holy, one of the ten commandments, commanding solemn rest and no work)
Mark 2:23-28

Thoughts and Notes:

_____

_____

_____

_____

_____

_____

_____

_____

_____

_____

_____

_____

_____

_____

Day 260

The parable of the sower
Mark 4:3-9

Reminder: A parable is a short story illustrating a moral lesson or religious principle.

The parable of the sower is explained
Mark 4:13-20

Thoughts and Notes:

_____

_____

_____

_____

_____

_____

_____

_____

_____

_____

_____

_____

_____

Day 261

The Pharisees value their traditions over God's commands
Mark 7:5-9

Jesus feeds 4,000 people
Mark 8:2-9

Thoughts and Notes:

_____

_____

_____

_____

_____

_____

_____

_____

_____

_____

_____

_____

_____

_____

_____

Day 262

Do good and be radical about not sinning
Mark 9:42-48

Jesus clears merchants from the Temple
Mark 11:15-17

Thoughts and Notes:

_____

_____

_____

_____

_____

_____

_____

_____

_____

_____

_____

_____

_____

_____

_____

Day 263

Forgive to be forgiven
Mark 11:25-26

The first and second greatest commandments
Mark 12:28-34

Thoughts and Notes:

_____

_____

_____

_____

_____

_____

_____

_____

_____

_____

_____

_____

_____

_____

_____

Day 264

Do not be lead astray, but be saved
Mark 13:5-13

Only the Father knows when Jesus will return
Mark 13:32-37

Thoughts and Notes:

_____

_____

_____

_____

_____

_____

_____

_____

_____

_____

_____

_____

_____

_____

_____

Day 265

A new covenant from Jesus
Mark 14:22-24

Jesus prays about his sufferings to come
Mark 14:35-36

Thoughts and Notes:

_____

_____

_____

_____

_____

_____

_____

_____

_____

_____

_____

_____

_____

Day 266

Jesus is mocked and beaten
Mark 15:17-20

Jesus dies on the cross
Mark 15:34-39

Thoughts and Notes:

_____

_____

_____

_____

_____

_____

_____

_____

_____

_____

_____

_____

_____

_____

Day 267

Jesus is risen from the dead
Mark 16:3-6

Jesus' final instructions
Mark 16:15-16

Jesus goes to Heaven
Mark 16:19

Thoughts and Notes:

_____

_____

_____

_____

_____

_____

_____

_____

_____

_____

_____

_____

_____

_____

Day 268

LUKE OVERVIEW

Title: Named after a believer of Jesus and a companion of Paul (Read II Timothy 4:11 "Luke alone is with me. Get Mark and bring him with you, for he is very useful to me for ministry.")

Author: Thought to be Luke

Audience: Theophilus (Read Luke 1:3)

Historical setting: During Jesus' life and after He was killed and rose from the dead. (Approximately 0-33 A.D.)

An angel's announcement to Mary
Luke 1:30-35

Thoughts and Notes:

_____

_____

_____

_____

_____

_____

_____

_____

_____

_____

Day 269

Jesus' birth announcement
Luke 2:8-14

Jesus at the age of 12
Luke 2:41-49

Thoughts and Notes:

_____

_____

_____

_____

_____

_____

_____

_____

_____

_____

_____

_____

_____

_____

_____

Day 270

John the Baptist prepares Jesus' way
Luke 3:2-6

Blessings and woes from Jesus
Luke 6:20-26

Thoughts and Notes:

_____

_____

_____

_____

_____

_____

_____

_____

_____

_____

_____

_____

_____

Day 271

Take the log out of your own eye first
Luke 6:39-42

People are known by their fruit
Luke 6:43-45

Thoughts and Notes:

_____

_____

_____

_____

_____

_____

_____

_____

_____

_____

_____

_____

_____

Day 272

Following Jesus
Luke 9:57-62

Either be rich for yourself or for God
Luke 12:15-21

Thoughts and Notes:

_____

_____

_____

_____

_____

_____

_____

_____

_____

_____

_____

_____

_____

_____

Day 273

Do not worry about basic needs
Luke 12:22-31

The rich man and Lazarus
Luke 16:19-31

Question for Thought: Do you feel there is any benefit to being anxious or worried? (Luke 12:22-31)

Thoughts and Notes:

_____

_____

_____

_____

_____

_____

_____

_____

_____

_____

_____

_____

Day 274

Thoughts and Notes:

_____

_____

_____

_____

_____

_____

_____

_____

_____

_____

_____

_____

_____

Day 275

Jesus on trial
Luke 22:66-71

Jesus on the cross
Luke 23:34-35

Thoughts and Notes:

_____

_____

_____

_____

_____

_____

_____

_____

_____

_____

_____

_____

_____

_____

Day 276

Jesus' last breath
Luke 23:46

Alive again, Jesus opens the minds of his disciples
Luke 24:44-48

Thoughts and Notes:

Day 277

JOHN OVERVIEW

Title: Named after one of Jesus' Twelve Disciples

Author: Thought to be John

Audience: The entire world

Historical setting: During Jesus' life and after he was killed and rose from the dead. (Approximately 0-33 A.D.)

Reminder: A disciple is one of Jesus' chosen 12 of inner circle followers/believers who accepted and helped spread Jesus' teachings.

The Word and the Light
John 1:1-14

Thoughts and Notes:

_____

_____

_____

_____

_____

_____

_____

Day 278

Jesus is the Lamb of God
John 1:29

21 Then Moses called all the elders of Israel and said to them, "Go and select lambs for yourselves according to your clans, and kill the Passover lamb. 22 Take a bunch of hyssop and dip it in the blood that is in the basin, and touch the lintel and the two doorposts with the blood that is in the basin. None of you shall go out of the door of his house until the morning. 23 For the Lord will pass through to strike the Egyptians, and when he sees the blood on the lintel and on the two doorposts, the Lord will pass over the door and will not allow the destroyer to enter your houses to strike you.
Exodus 12:21-23

You must be born again
John 3:1-8

Thoughts and Notes:

_____

_____

_____

_____

_____

_____

_____

_____

_____

Day 279

God loves the people in the world
John 3:16-18

The Father and Son's relationship
John 5:18-24

Thoughts and Notes:

_____

_____

_____

_____

_____

_____

_____

_____

_____

_____

_____

_____

_____

_____

Day 280

Jesus walks on water
John 6:16-20

Seek eternal food
John 6:25-27

Thoughts and Notes:

_____

_____

_____

_____

_____

_____

_____

_____

_____

_____

_____

_____

_____

_____

_____

Day 281

The merciful judgment of an adulteress
John 8:3-11

10 "If a man commits adultery with the wife of his neighbor, both the adulterer and the adulteress shall surely be put to death.
Leviticus 20:10

Question for Thought: Why do you think the scribes and Pharisees did not stone the woman and walked away when Jesus told them, "whoever has no sin can be the first to throw a stone at her"? (John 8:3-11)

Thoughts and Notes:

_____

_____

_____

_____

_____

_____

_____

_____

_____

_____

_____

_____

Day 282

Believe the works
John 10:31-38

The resurrection and life is Jesus
John 11:21-25

Jesus is the example
John 13:12-17

Thoughts and Notes:

_____

_____

_____

_____

_____

_____

_____

_____

_____

_____

_____

_____

_____

Day 283

A new commandment
John 13:34-35

The people who love Jesus
John 14:21-24

Thoughts and Notes:

_____

_____

_____

_____

_____

_____

_____

_____

_____

_____

_____

_____

_____

_____

Day 284

Jesus tells the disciples to ask of the Father
John 16:23

Jesus thought of his mother, while dying on the cross
John 19:25-27

Thoughts and Notes:

_____

_____

_____

_____

_____

_____

_____

_____

_____

_____

_____

_____

Day 285

Believe
John 20:24-31

Jesus did a lot more
John 21:25

Thoughts and Notes:

_____

_____

_____

_____

_____

_____

_____

_____

_____

_____

_____

_____

_____

Day 286

ACTS OVERVIEW

Title: Named after the various deeds or "acts" that the Apostles performed after Jesus ascended to Heaven (Read Acts 1:13-14)

Note: An apostle is a follower of Jesus who now is a leader and preacher to fellow believers. (Read 1 Corinthians 12:28 "28 And God has appointed in the church first apostles, second prophets, third teachers, then miracles, then gifts of healing, helping, administrating, and various kinds of tongues.")

Author: No absolute scripture says who the author is, although it was the same person who wrote Luke, so most believe it was Luke (Read Acts 1:1-2)

Audience: Theophilus

Historical setting: Directly after Jesus' death and resurrection for about the next 30 years (as Paul's, an apostle, journeys and events mention) (Approximately 44-70 A.D.)

The Holy Spirit will come when Jesus leaves
Acts 1:4-11

Thoughts and Notes:

_____

_____

_____

_____

_____

Day 287

Peter testifies about Jesus
Acts 2:32-33

3,000 souls are saved
Acts 2:40-41

Thoughts and Notes:

_____

_____

_____

_____

_____

_____

_____

_____

_____

_____

_____

_____

_____

_____

_____

Day 288

Peter heals a lame man
Acts 3:2-8

Peter and John arrested for healing the lame man
Acts 4:3-12

Thoughts and Notes:

_____

_____

_____

_____

_____

_____

_____

_____

_____

_____

_____

_____

_____

_____

Day 289

Prison does not stop the Apostles from witnessing about Jesus
Acts 5:17-25

Stephen is killed for witnessing to Israel's leaders
Acts 7:48-60

Thoughts and Notes:

_____

_____

_____

_____

_____

_____

_____

_____

_____

_____

_____

_____

_____

_____

_____

Day 290

Saul, a persecutor of the church, meets Jesus
Acts 9:1-6

The Gentiles receive the Holy Spirit
Acts 10:44-47

Note: Gentiles are people who are not Jewish/Israelites.

Question for Thought: God used a bright light to get Saul's attention. Do you think it is possible for God to use unique ways to get our attention today? (Acts 9:1-6)

Thoughts and Notes:

_____

_____

_____

_____

_____

_____

_____

_____

_____

_____

_____

_____

Day 291

Saul is to go by the name of Paul
Acts 13:9

The Bereans studied scripture rather than only believing Paul
Acts 17:11-12

Thoughts and Notes:

_____

_____

_____

_____

_____

_____

_____

_____

_____

_____

_____

_____

_____

_____

_____

Day 292

Know Jesus to cast out demons
Acts 19:11-17

Paul defends his faith
Acts 24:16-21

Thoughts and Notes:

_____

_____

_____

_____

_____

_____

_____

_____

_____

_____

_____

_____

_____

_____

Day 293

ROMANS OVERVIEW

Title: Named after the people it was written to (Read Romans 1:7)

Author: Paul (Read Romans 1:1)

Audience: The people in Rome

Historical setting: During Paul's ministry. (Approximately 55-57 A.D.)

Thoughts and Notes:

_____
_____
_____
_____
_____
_____
_____
_____
_____
_____
_____
_____
_____
_____

Day 294

All know there is a God
Romans 1:16-20

More evidence there is a God
Romans 2:13-16

Question for Thought: The Bible states that those who do not believe in God are without excuse because God has shown himself to them. If this is true then why are there "non-believers"? (Romans 1:16-20)

Thoughts and Notes:

_____

_____

_____

_____

_____

_____

_____

_____

_____

_____

_____

_____

Day 295

ll have sinned but can be forgiven
Romans 3:21-23

Think in the spirit, not the flesh
Romans 8:1-6

Thoughts and Notes:

_____

_____

_____

_____

_____

_____

_____

_____

_____

_____

_____

_____

_____

_____

Day 296

Faith comes by hearing
Romans 10:14-17

How to know God's will
Romans 12:1-2

Question for Thought: Do you confess that Jesus is your lord and believe that God raised Jesus from the dead? (Romans 10:9)

Thoughts and Notes:

_____

_____

_____

_____

_____

_____

_____

_____

_____

_____

_____

_____

_____

Day 297

Love fulfills the law
Romans 13:8-10

The mystery of God is revealed
Romans 16:25-27

Thoughts and Notes:

_____

_____

_____

_____

_____

_____

_____

_____

_____

_____

_____

_____

_____

Day 298

I CORINTHIANS OVERVIEW

Title: Named after the people it was written to (Read I Corinthians 1:2)

Author: Paul (Read I Corinthians 1:1)

Audience: The church at Corinth

Historical setting: During Paul's ministry. (Approximately 53-55 A.D.)

A plea for no dissention of believers
I Corinthians 1:10

Thoughts and Notes:

_____

_____

_____

_____

_____

_____

_____

_____

_____

_____

_____

_____

Day 299

Wisdom of the mysteries of God
I Corinthians 2:6-10

The temple of God's spirit
I Corinthians 3:16-17

Thoughts and Notes:

_____

_____

_____

_____

_____

_____

_____

_____

_____

_____

_____

_____

_____

_____

Day 300

Do not take a brother to a worldly court
I Corinthians 6:1-3

Preachers are worthy of a salary
I Corinthians 9:9-11

Thoughts and Notes:

_____

_____

_____

_____

_____

_____

_____

_____

_____

_____

_____

_____

_____

_____

_____

_____

Day 301

Instructions for the Lord's Supper
I Corinthians 11:23-26

Love is the greatest gift
I Corinthians 13:1-13

Thoughts and Notes:

_____

_____

_____

_____

_____

_____

_____

_____

_____

_____

_____

_____

_____

_____

Day 302

Tongues and prophecy
I Corinthians 14:20-25

Note: Tongues is a spiritual gift from God manifested as a vocal utterance.

7 To each is given the manifestation of the Spirit for the common good. 8 For to one is given through the Spirit the utterance of wisdom, and to another the utterance of knowledge according to the same Spirit, 9 to another faith by the same Spirit, to another gifts of healing by the one Spirit, 10 to another the working of miracles, to another prophecy, to another the ability to distinguish between spirits, to another various kinds of tongues, to another the interpretation of tongues.
I Corinthians 12:7-11

Thoughts and Notes:

_____

_____

_____

_____

_____

_____

_____

_____

_____

_____

_____

Day 303

Hope is in Christ's resurrection
I Corinthians 15:17-22

The resurrection of the dead
I Corinthians 15:42-44

Thoughts and Notes:

_____

_____

_____

_____

_____

_____

_____

_____

_____

_____

_____

_____

_____

_____

Day 304

II CORINTHIANS OVERVIEW

Title: Named for the second time Paul wrote to the church at Corinth

Author: Paul (Read II Corinthians 1:1)

Audience: The church at Corinth

Historical setting: Before Paul's third visit to Corinth (Approximately 55-56 A.D.)

Using God's comfort to help others through hard times
II Corinthians 1:3-5

Do not lose heart
II Corinthians 4:13-18

Thoughts and Notes:

_____

_____

_____

_____

_____

_____

_____

Day 305

Walk by faith
II Corinthians 5:6-10

Be separate from unbelievers
II Corinthians 6:14-18

Thoughts and Notes:

_____

_____

_____

_____

_____

_____

_____

_____

_____

_____

_____

_____

_____

_____

Day 306

War in the spirit
II Corinthians 10:3-6

Paul's past tribulations
II Corinthians 11:24-28

Thoughts and Notes:

_____

_____

_____

_____

_____

_____

_____

_____

_____

_____

_____

_____

_____

_____

Day 307

Strength in weakness
II Corinthians 12:7-10

Paul's goodbye
II Corinthians 13:11-14

Thoughts and Notes:

_____

_____

_____

_____

_____

_____

_____

_____

_____

_____

_____

_____

_____

_____

Day 308

GALATIANS OVERVIEW

Title: Named for the people it was written to (Read Galatians 1:1-2)

Author: Paul

Audience: The churches in Galatia

Historical setting: Paul had his ministry during Peter's (also known as Cephas) and knew him (Read Galatians 1:18). (Approximately 47-48 A.D.)

Jesus had siblings while on the Earth
Galatians 1:19

31 And his mother and his brothers came, and standing outside they sent to him and called him. 32 And a crowd was sitting around him, and they said to him, "Your mother and your brothers are outside, seeking you." 33 And he answered them, "Who are my mother and my brothers?" 34 And looking about at those who sat around him, he said, "Here are my mother and my brothers! 35 For whoever does the will of God, he is my brother and sister and mother."
Mark 3:31-35

Thoughts and Notes:

_____

_____

_____

_____

_____

_____

Day 309

Justified by faith with Abraham
Galatians 3:7-9

All are one in Christ
Galatians 3:28-29

Thoughts and Notes:

_____

_____

_____

_____

_____

_____

_____

_____

_____

_____

_____

_____

_____

_____

Day 310

Heirs with Christ
Galatians 4:4-7

Walk in the spirit, not in the flesh
Galatians 5:17-25

Thoughts and Notes:

_____

_____

_____

_____

_____

_____

_____

_____

_____

_____

_____

_____

_____

_____

Day 311

EPHESIANS OVERVIEW

Title: Named for the people it was written to (Read Ephesians 1:1)

Author: Paul

Audience: The saints (believers in Jesus) in Ephesus

Historical setting: Paul wrote this while he was in prison.
        (Approximately 60-62 A.D.)

Saved by grace through faith
Ephesians 2:4-9

Thoughts and Notes:

_____

_____

_____

_____

_____

_____

_____

_____

_____

_____

Day 312

Being spiritually mature
Ephesians 4:11-15

Behave like God
Ephesians 5:1-8

Thoughts and Notes:

_____

_____

_____

_____

_____

_____

_____

_____

_____

_____

_____

_____

_____

_____

_____

Day 313

Wives and husbands
Ephesians 5:22-33

Children and their parents
Ephesians 6:1-4

Thoughts and Notes:

_____

_____

_____

_____

_____

_____

_____

_____

_____

_____

_____

_____

_____

_____

Day 314

PHILIPPIANS OVERVIEW

Title: Named for the people it was written to (Read Philippians 1:1)

Author: Paul

Audience: The saints (believers), bishops, and deacons (leaders in the church) in Philippi

Historical setting: Paul was in prison when he wrote this also (Read Philippians 1:12-13). (Approximately 60-61 A.D.)

To live or die for Jesus is good
Philippians 1:21-24

Thoughts and Notes:

_____

_____

_____

_____

_____

_____

_____

_____

_____

_____

Day 315

Have the mind of Jesus
Philippians 2:4-8

Press toward the goal
Philippians 3:12-14

Thoughts and Notes:

_____

_____

_____

_____

_____

_____

_____

_____

_____

_____

_____

_____

_____

_____

_____

Day 316

Question for Thought: This Scripture tells us what to have our thoughts on. Do you feel thinking this way would be beneficial for people today? (Philippians 4:6-8)

Thoughts and Notes:

_____

_____

_____

_____

_____

_____

_____

_____

_____

_____

_____

_____

_____

Day 317

COLOSSIANS OVERVIEW

Title: Named for the people it was written to (Read Colossians 1:1-2)

Author: Paul

Audience: The saints and faithful brothers in Colossae (spelling various between different Bible translations).

Historical setting: Paul wrote this in prison also, and had a fellow prisoner (Read Colossians 4:10 "Aristarchus my fellow prisoner greets you, and Mark the cousin of Barnabas (concerning whom you have received instructions—if he comes to you, welcome him),"). (Approximately 62 A.D.)

Thoughts and Notes:

_____

_____

_____

_____

_____

_____

_____

_____

_____

_____

Day 318

Who Jesus is and His purpose
Colossians 1:15-20

Not men's ideas, but Christ
Colossians 2:8

Thoughts and Notes:

_____

_____

_____

_____

_____

_____

_____

_____

_____

_____

_____

_____

_____

_____

Day 319

Put your sinful body to death
Colossians 3:4-6

Do all in the name of Jesus Christ
Colossians 3:16-17

Thoughts and Notes:

_____

_____

_____

_____

_____

_____

_____

_____

_____

_____

_____

_____

Day 320

I THESSALONIANS OVERVIEW

Title: Named for the people it was written to (Read I Thessalonians 1:1)

Author: Paul

Audience: The church of Thessalonica

Historical setting: Paul wrote this after he had spent time with the Thessalonians. (Approximately 49-52 A.D.)

Hope and being with the Lord and loved ones
I Thessalonians 4:13-18

Thoughts and Notes:

_____

_____

_____

_____

_____

_____

_____

_____

_____

Day 321

Watch for the Lord's returning
I Thessalonians 5:2-6

Instructions for life
I Thessalonians 5:14-22

Question for Thought: This Scripture suggests to "stay alert" for Christ's second coming. His first coming was over two thousands ago; do you think the second coming is going to happen soon or at all? (I Thessalonians 5:2-6)

Thoughts and Notes:

_____

_____

_____

_____

_____

_____

_____

_____

_____

_____

Day 322

Title: Named for the people this second letter was written to

Author: Paul

Audience: The church of Thessalonica

Historical setting: Paul wrote this while he was with his friends and fellow believers, Silvanus and Timothy. (Read II Thessalonians 1:1) (40-51 A.D.)

Being worthy of God through afflictions
II Thessalonians 1:4-7

Thoughts and Notes:

_____

_____

_____

_____

_____

_____

_____

_____

_____

Day 323

Do not be deceived by lying wonders
II Thessalonians 2:7-10

"If a prophet or a dreamer of dreams arises among you and gives you a sign or a wonder, 2 and the sign or wonder that he tells you comes to pass, and if he says, 'Let us go after other gods,' which you have not known, 'and let us serve them,' 3 you shall not listen to the words of that prophet or that dreamer of dreams. For the Lord your God is testing you, to know whether you love the Lord your God with all your heart and with all your soul.
Deuteronomy 13:1-3

If anyone will not work they shall not eat
II Thessalonians 3:10-12

Thoughts and Notes:

_____

_____

_____

_____

_____

_____

_____

_____

_____

_____

Day 324

I TIMOTHY OVERVIEW

Title: Named for the person it was written to

Author: Paul

Audience: Timothy (Read I Timothy 1:1-2)

Historical setting: Paul wrote this to a young man, Timothy (a disciple of Jesus) (Read I Timothy 4:12 "Let no one despise you for your youth, but set the believers an example in speech, in conduct, in love, in faith, in purity."). (Approximately 59-62 A.D.)

Paul is forgiven for persecuting the church
I Timothy 1:13-15

Thoughts and Notes:

_____

_____

_____

_____

_____

_____

_____

_____

Day 325

Men's prayer and women's apparel
I Timothy 2:8-10

Qualifications for Deacons
I Timothy 3:8-12

Thoughts and Notes:

_____

_____

_____

_____

_____

_____

_____

_____

_____

_____

_____

_____

_____

_____

_____

Day 326

The great mystery of godliness
I Timothy 3:16

Deceitful demons
I Timothy 4:1-5

Thoughts and Notes:

_____

_____

_____

_____

_____

_____

_____

_____

_____

_____

_____

_____

_____

_____

Day 327

Instructions for rebuking others
I Timothy 5:1-2

Instructions for rich people
I Timothy 6:17-19

Thoughts and Notes:

_____

_____

_____

_____

_____

_____

_____

_____

_____

_____

_____

_____

_____

Day 328

II TIMOTHY OVERVIEW

Title: Named because this is the second letter written to Timothy

Author: Paul

Audience: Timothy (Read II Timothy 1:1-2)

Historical setting: During Paul's continued ministry. (Approximately 63 A.D)

Run the race of life strongly
II Timothy 2:3-7

Thoughts and Notes:

_____

_____

_____

_____

_____

_____

_____

_____

_____

_____

Day 329

Be approved to God
II Timothy 2:15-16

Evil people in the Last Days
II Timothy 3:1-5

Where scripture comes from
II Timothy 3:16-17

Question for Thought: Do you think the Bible is used today for teaching and training in mainly positive or negative uses? (II Timothy 3:16-17)

Thoughts and Notes:

_____

_____

_____

_____

_____

_____

_____

_____

_____

Day 330

TITUS OVERVIEW

Title: Named for the person it was written to.

Author: Paul (Read Titus 1:1)

Audience: Titus (Read Titus 1:4)

Historical setting: Titus was a trusted companion of Paul
(Approximately 60-66 A.D.)

False, corrupt teachers in church
Titus 1:10-16

Thoughts and Notes:

_____

_____

_____

_____

_____

_____

_____

_____

_____

_____

©2013 Basic Bible Guide

Day 331

Instruct and live as a truthful teacher
Titus 2:1-8

Obey authorities and show courtesy toward all people
Titus 3:1-2

Thoughts and Notes:

_____

_____

_____

_____

_____

_____

_____

_____

_____

_____

_____

_____

_____

_____

Day 332

PHILEMON OVERVIEW

Title: Named for the person it was written to

Author: Paul and Timothy

Audience: Philemon

Historical setting: Paul wrote this while he was in prison (Read
Philemon 1:1). (Approximately 60-62 A.D)

Prayers and joy for a brother in the faith
Philemon 1:4-7

Paul sends back a slave who has become a believer in Jesus
Philemon 1:13-16

Thoughts and Notes:

_____

_____

_____

_____

_____

_____

_____

_____

©2013 Basic Bible Guide

Day 333

HEBREWS OVERVIEW

Title: Named for the people it was written to

Author: There is none referenced

Audience: By all the references made to the Jewish laws, found in the Old Testament, and to the word "us" in Hebrews Chapter 10, it can be reasoned this letter is to the Hebrew/Jewish believers of Jesus

Historical setting: While Timothy was still living (Read Hebrews 13:23 "You should know that our brother Timothy has been released, with whom I shall see you if he comes soon). (Approximately 65-70 A.D.)

Jesus' relationship to angels
Hebrews 1:1-5

1 The Lord says to my Lord:
 "Sit at my right hand,
until I make your enemies your footstool."
Psalm 110:1

Do not neglect salvation
Hebrews 2:3-4

Thoughts and Notes:

_____

_____

_____

_____

347

Day 334

Do not harden your heart
Hebrews 3:7-9

6 Oh come, let us worship and bow down;
   let us kneel before the Lord, our Maker!
7 For he is our God,
   and we are the people of his pasture,
   and the sheep of his hand.
Today, if you hear his voice,
8   do not harden your hearts, as at Meribah,
   as on the day at Massah in the wilderness,
9 when your fathers put me to the test
   and put me to the proof, though they had seen my work.
10 For forty years I loathed that generation
   and said, "They are a people who go astray in their heart,
   and they have not known my ways."
11 Therefore I swore in my wrath,
   "They shall not enter my rest."
Psalm 95:6-11

The Word of God is alive
Hebrews 4:11-13

Thoughts and Notes:

_____

_____

_____

_____

_____

_____

Day 335

Jesus the High Priest sympathizes with people
Hebrews 4:14-16

15 "Then he shall kill the goat of the sin offering that is for the people and bring its blood inside the veil and do with its blood as he did with the blood of the bull, sprinkling it over the mercy seat and in front of the mercy seat.
Leviticus 16:15

Jesus and Melchizedek
(*Only read these 2 verses*)
Hebrews 6:19, 7:3

A New Covenant
Hebrews 8:7-13

Thoughts and Notes:

_____

_____

_____

_____

_____

_____

_____

_____

_____

_____

Day 336

Christ the High Priest
Hebrews 9:11-12

Christ's blood is the final sacrifice
Hebrews 9:24-28

Aaron shall make atonement on its horns once a year. With the blood of the sin offering of atonement he shall make atonement for it once in the year throughout your generations. It is most holy to the Lord."
Exodus 30:6-10

The explanation of faith
Hebrews 10:38-11:1

The faith of Enoch and Noah (from the Old Testament)
Hebrews 11:5-7

Thoughts and Notes:

_____

_____

_____

_____

_____

_____

_____

_____

Day 337

The faith of Abraham, Isaac, Jacob, and Joseph (from the Old Testament)
Hebrews 11:17-22

More examples of faith from the Old Testament
Hebrews 11:29-35

Come to Mount Zion
Hebrews 12:22-23

Thoughts and Notes:

_____

_____

_____

_____

_____

_____

_____

_____

_____

_____

_____

_____

Day 338

Entertaining angels
Hebrews 13:1-2

Be content and fearless
Hebrews 13:5-6

Offer a sacrifice of praise
Hebrews 13:14-15

Thoughts and Notes:

_____

_____

_____

_____

_____

_____

_____

_____

_____

_____

_____

_____

©2013 Basic Bible Guide

Day 339

JAMES OVERVIEW

Title: Named for the author of this book

Author: James (Read James 1:1)

Audience: The twelve tribes of Israel

Reminder: Jacob's name was changed to Israel, his 12 sons and their offspring became the 12 tribes of Israel.

Historical setting: James is believed to be a sibling of Jesus (Read Matthew 13:55 "Is this not the carpenter's son? Is not His mother called Mary? And His brothers James, Joses, Simon and Judas?"). (Between 40-47 A.D.)

Trials and wisdom
James 1:2-8

Thoughts and Notes:

_____

_____

_____

_____

_____

_____

_____

353

Day 340

A crown, temptations, and good gifts
James 1:12-17

Be doers, not just hearers
James 1:22-27

Thoughts and Notes:

_____

_____

_____

_____

_____

_____

_____

_____

_____

_____

_____

_____

_____

_____

_____

Day 341

Faith without works is dead
James 2:14-22

Where fights and wars come from
James 4:1-3

Trust God's will without boasting
James 4:13-17

Thoughts and Notes:

_____
_____
_____
_____
_____
_____
_____
_____
_____
_____
_____

Day 342

Be patient
James 5:7-8

Persevere like Job
James 5:11

Pray if troubled, sing if cheerful, confess if sinful
James 5:13-16

Thoughts and Notes:

_____

_____

_____

_____

_____

_____

_____

_____

_____

_____

_____

_____

Day 343

I PETER OVERVIEW

Title: Named for this first of two letters to various believers

Author: Peter

Reminder: Peter was one of the original twelve men selected by Jesus to assist him in his ministry, he was also known as a disciple or apostle.

Audience: The fellow believers seeking refuge from religious persecution in numerous locations (Read I Peter 1:1)

Historical setting: By this time the Christians were widespread. (Approximately 54-68 A.D.)

Salvation and a reason why trials come
I Peter 1:3-9

Thoughts and Notes:

_____

_____

_____

_____

_____

_____

Day 344

Born again of incorruptible seed
I Peter 1:22-25

Wives and disobedient husbands
I Peter 3:1-4

Instruction for husbands
I Peter 3:7

Question for Thought: What does being "born again" mean? (1 Peter 1:22-23)

Thoughts and Notes:

_____

_____

_____

_____

_____

_____

_____

_____

_____

_____

_____

Day 345

Be ready to answer for your hope
I Peter 3:15

Blessing in suffering for Christ
I Peter 4:14-16

Resist the devil
I Peter 5:8-9

7 Submit yourselves therefore to God. Resist the devil, and he will flee from you. 8 Draw near to God, and he will draw near to you. Cleanse your hands, you sinners, and purify your hearts, you double-minded.
James 4:7-8

Thoughts and Notes:

_____

_____

_____

_____

_____

_____

_____

_____

_____

Day 346

Title: Named for the author's second letter

Author: Peter

Audience: Those of the faith (Read II Peter 1:1)

Historical setting: Peter wrote this near his death (Read II Peter 1:13-14). (Approximately 64-67 A.D.)

Add to your faith
II Peter 1:5-8

True prophesies come from God
II Peter 1:19-2:1

Thoughts and Notes:

_____

_____

_____

_____

_____

_____

_____

_____

Day 347

The Lord knows how to deliver the Righteous
II Peter 2:4-9

The two angels came to Sodom in the evening, and Lot was sitting in the gate of Sodom. When Lot saw them, he rose to meet them and bowed himself with his face to the earth 2 and said, "My lords, please turn aside to your servant's house and spend the night and wash your feet. Then you may rise up early and go on your way." They said, "No; we will spend the night in the town square." 3 But he pressed them strongly; so they turned aside to him and entered his house. And he made them a feast and baked unleavened bread, and they ate.

4 But before they lay down, the men of the city, the men of Sodom, both young and old, all the people to the last man, surrounded the house. 5 And they called to Lot, "Where are the men who came to you tonight? Bring them out to us, that we may know them." 6 Lot went out to the men at the entrance, shut the door after him, 7 and said, "I beg you, my brothers, do not act so wickedly. 8 Behold, I have two daughters who have not known any man. Let me bring them out to you, and do to them as you please. Only do nothing to these men, for they have come under the shelter of my roof." 9 But they said, "Stand back!" And they said, "This fellow came to sojourn, and he has become the judge! Now we will deal worse with you than with them." Then they pressed hard against the man Lot, and drew near to break the door down. 10 But the men reached out their hands and brought Lot into the house with them and shut the door. 11 And they struck with blindness the men who were at the entrance of the house, both small and great, so that they wore themselves out groping for the door. 12 Then the men said to Lot, "Have you anyone else here? Sons-in-law, sons, daughters, or anyone you have in the city, bring them out of the place. 13 For we are about to destroy this place, because the outcry against its people has become great before the LORD, and the LORD has sent us to destroy it."

Genesis 19:1-13

Repent, the Lord will return
II Peter 3:8-10

Thoughts and Notes:

_____

_____

_____

Day 348

Title: Named for the assumed author

Author: Thought to be John (one of the 12 disciples of Jesus), but no exact reference is given

Audience: The author's fellow believers (Read I John 2:1)

Historical setting: This book was written by someone who physically knew Jesus (Read I John 1:1) (Approximately 67-90 A.D.)

Walk in the Light and confess your sins
I John 1:6-10

Question for Thought: Is there any value to confessing our sins? (1 John 1:5-10)

Thoughts and Notes:

_____

_____

_____

_____

_____

_____

_____

Day 349

If you hate your brother you are in darkness
I John 2:9-11

Do not love the world
I John 2:15-16

4 But the serpent said to the woman, "You will not surely die. 5 For God knows that when you eat of it your eyes will be opened, and you will be like God, knowing good and evil." 6 So when the woman saw that the tree was good for food, and that it was a delight to the eyes, and that the tree was to be desired to make one wise, she took of its fruit and ate, and she also gave some to her husband who was with her, and he ate. 7 Then the eyes of both were opened, and they knew that they were naked. And they sewed fig leaves together and made themselves loincloths.
Genesis 3:4-7

Thoughts and Notes:

Day 350

Test the spirits
I John 4:1-4

Perfect love casts out fear
I John 4:17-19

7 for God gave us a spirit not of fear but of power and love and self-control.
II Timothy 1:7

Thoughts and Notes:

_____

_____

_____

_____

_____

_____

_____

_____

_____

_____

_____

_____

_____

© 2013 Basic Bible Guide

Day 351

Confidence in prayer
I John 5:14-15

The world lies under the control the wicked one
I John 5:19-20

Thoughts and Notes:

_____

_____

_____

_____

_____

_____

_____

_____

_____

_____

_____

_____

_____

365

Day 352

II JOHN OVERVIEW

Title: Named after the assumed author (his second letter)

Author: "the Elder"

Audience: The elect lady and her children (Read II John 1:1)

Historical setting: A couple decades after Jesus died, resurrected and ascended into Heaven (Read II John 1:7). (Approximately 67-90 A.D.)

Watch for false teachers and false believers
II John 1:8-11

Thoughts and Notes:

_____

_____

_____

_____

_____

_____

_____

_____

_____

Day 353

III JOHN OVERVIEW

Title: Named after the assumed author's third book.

Author: "the Elder"

Audience: Gaius (Read III John 1:1)

Historical setting: A couple decades after Jesus died, resurrected and ascended into Heaven. There were lovers of power in the church then (Read III John 1:9). (Approximately 67-90 A.D.)

Encouragement to walk in the truth
III John 1:2-4

Thoughts and Notes:

_____

_____

_____

_____

_____

_____

_____

_____

Day 354

JUDE OVERVIEW

Title: Named after the author

Author: Jude

Audience: Those who are called and believe in Jesus (Read Jude 1:1)

Historical setting: A couple decades after Jesus died, resurrected and ascended into Heaven.

(Approximately 60-72 A.D.)

The character and doom of godless men
Jude 1:5-11

Beware, pray, and save people
Jude 1:18-23

Thoughts and Notes:

_____

_____

_____

_____

_____

_____

_____

Day 355

REVELATION OVERVIEW

Title: Named due to events "revealed" to John by Jesus Christ

Author: John (Read Revelation 1:1)

Audience: The seven churches in Asia (Read Revelation 1:4)

Historical setting: This book covers messages to the churches, the judgment of the world, as well as visions of the future and extends to the end of this world and the beginning of a new one (Read Revelation 21:1 "Then I saw a new heaven and a new earth, for the first heaven and the first earth had passed away, and the sea was no more."). (Approximately 68 A.D. to the last days of this world)

Thoughts and Notes:

_____

_____

_____

_____

_____

_____

_____

_____

_____

_____

Day 356

9 And when he had said these things, as they were looking on, he was lifted up, and a cloud took him out of their sight. 10 And while they were gazing into heaven as he went, behold, two men stood by them in white robes, 11 and said, "Men of Galilee, why do you stand looking into heaven? This Jesus, who was taken up from you into heaven, will come in the same way as you saw him go into heaven."

Acts 1:9-11

A letter to the churches from Jesus
Revelation 3:15-22

Thoughts and Notes:

_____

_____

_____

_____

_____

_____

_____

_____

_____

_____

Day 357

The Lamb is worthy to open the scroll
Revelation 5:5-10

The sixth seal of God's judgment is opened
Revelation 6:12-17

Many people in Heaven from every nation
Revelation 7:9-12

Thoughts and Notes:

_____

_____

_____

_____

_____

_____

_____

_____

_____

_____

_____

Day 358

The seven trumpets
Revelation 8:2-6

The sixth trumpet
Revelation 9:15-21

The two witnesses
Revelation 11:3-12

Thoughts and Notes:

_____

_____

_____

_____

_____

_____

_____

_____

_____

_____

_____

_____

Day 359

The Archangel Michael and his angels fight against Satan and his angels
Revelation 12:7-12

The beast and the dragon
Revelation 13:1-9

Note: A diadem is another word used for a crown.

Thoughts and Notes:

_____

_____

_____

_____

_____

_____

_____

_____

_____

_____

_____

_____

_____

Day 360

The second beast
Revelation 13:11-18

The mark of the beast
Revelation 14:9-12

The last seven plagues in bowls
Revelation 15:1-4

Thoughts and Notes:

_____

_____

_____

_____

_____

_____

_____

_____

_____

_____

_____

_____

Day 361

The first bowl of wrath
Revelation 16:2

The seventh bowl of wrath
Revelation 16:13-18

Babylon, the woman on the beast
Revelation 17:3-7

Thoughts and Notes:

_____

_____

_____

_____

_____

_____

_____

_____

_____

_____

_____

_____

Day 362

An army of Heaven on white horses
Revelation 19:11-14

The great white throne; judgment
Revelation 20:11-15

A new Heaven and a new Earth with no more weeping or death
Revelation 21:1-4

Thoughts and Notes:

_____

_____

_____

_____

_____

_____

_____

_____

_____

_____

_____

_____

Day 363

Jesus is coming quickly
Revelation 22:16-21

1 "Let not your hearts be troubled. Believe in God; believe also in me. 2 In my Father's house are many rooms. If it were not so, would I have told you that I go to prepare a place for you? 3 And if I go and prepare a place for you, I will come again and will take you to myself, that where I am you may be also. 4 And you know the way to where I am going." 5 Thomas said to him, "Lord, we do not know where you are going. How can we know the way?" 6 Jesus said to him, "I am the way, and the truth, and the life. No one comes to the Father except through me.
John 14:1-6

Thoughts and Notes:

_____

_____

_____

_____

_____

_____

_____

_____

_____

_____

_____

Day 364

Note: This passage is an additional cross-reference to day 363 (Revelation 22:16-21).

---

8 But what does it say? "The word is near you, in your mouth and in your heart" (that is, the word of faith that we proclaim); 9 because, if you confess with your mouth that Jesus is Lord and believe in your heart that God raised him from the dead, you will be saved. 10 For with the heart one believes and is justified, and with the mouth one confesses and is saved. 11 For the Scripture says, "Everyone who believes in him will not be put to shame." 12 For there is no distinction between Jew and Greek; for the same Lord is Lord of all, bestowing his riches on all who call on him. 13 For "everyone who calls on the name of the Lord will be saved."

Romans 10:8-13

Thoughts and Notes:

Day 365

Note: This passage is an additional cross-reference to day 363 (Revelation 22:16-21).

25 And behold, a lawyer stood up to put him to the test, saying, "Teacher, what shall I do to inherit eternal life?" 26 He said to him, "What is written in the Law? How do you read it?" 27 And he answered, "You shall love the Lord your God with all your heart and with all your soul and with all your strength and with all your mind, and your neighbor as yourself." 28 And he said to him, "You have answered correctly; do this, and you will live."

Luke 10:25-28

Thoughts and Notes:

Congratulations on completing this devotional.

The folks at **BASIC BIBLE GUIDE** would love to hear what you thought of this program.

Please visit our website to leave your opinion:

www.BasicBibleGuide.org

Or write to:

2140 Academy Cir. Ste. C
Colorado Springs, CO 80909

For information to start a group with the Basic Bible Guide book that takes you through this program in "12 Simple 60 Minute Sessions", please visit our website.

To receive a free Certificate of Completion please email us at: info@BasicBibleGuide.org

Basic Bible Guide (BBG) exists to help people find out what the Bible says for themselves, regardless of their beliefs, with a fact-based, easy to use format.

Would you assist us and donate at least 1 dollar a month to translate BBG for people around the world?

Simply visit the "Donate" page of our website:
www.BasicBibleGuide.org

Thank You